W9-CCN-354

empowered

JOSH BERNOFF

TED SCHADLER

Forrester Research

empowered

unleash
your employees

energize
your customers

transform
your business

Harvard Business Review Press • Boston, Massachusetts

Library of Congress Cataloging-in-Publication Data

Bernoff, Josh.
    Empowered : unleash your employees, energize your customers, and transform your business / by Josh Bernoff and Ted Schadler.
        p. cm.
    ISBN 978-1-4221-5563-9 (hardcover : alk. paper)
1. Technological innovations—Management.   2. Business enterprises—Technological innovations.   3. Customer services—Technological innovations.   4. Online social networks—Economic aspects.   I. Schadler, Ted.   II. Title.
    HD45.B412 2010
    658.4'038—dc22

                                                                    2010012427

For George Forrester Colony,

who has inspired so many HEROes

contents

part one

HEROes

1. why your business needs HEROes

When Dooce rants, it's sheer poetry. Breathtaking in honesty and scope, Dooce's rants about motherhood have a quality that people appreciate, especially other mothers. You do *not* want to be the target of one of those rants.

Dooce is a thirty-four-year-old woman named Heather Armstrong. In August of 2009 she reached the end of her tether. Marlo, Heather's second child, had arrived two months earlier, in June. Heather knew what new babies mean: lots and lots of laundry. Her old Kenmore washer was failing. So she bought the big, heavy-duty clothes washer from Maytag, the company that for decades has advertised its dependability, and on top of that, she bought the ten-year warranty.

Twelve weeks into the life of baby number two, the Maytag was not doing its dependability thing. Heather's poetic rants appear on her blog, at dooce.com. Here's an excerpt from her rant about the Maytag, titled "Containing a capital letter or two":[1]

So, yeah. The damn thing broke a week after it was delivered. Started giving us this error reading and wouldn't fill up with water . . . So we called, complained, and they sent out a repairman. He shows up three days later and is all, yeah, gonna have to order parts. That's going to take another seven to ten days.

In the meantime, if we wanted to get a load of laundry done, we had to jury-rig the thing, reach our hand up and inside a certain compartment and jiggle a part. And then maybe it might work. Or not. We never knew . . . WE HAD TO JURY-RIG A $1,300 BRAND NEW WASHING MACHINE. Please tell me you're shaking your head. Right? RIGHT?

I've got a pile of milk-stained shirts sitting in a corner, SPOILING, because that's what milk does, IT SPOILS, CAN YOU EVEN IMAGINE THE SMELL. And an Olympic Baby Pooper. Onesie after onesie after onesie stacking up in the washroom, six pairs of Jon's pants stained, several pairs of my shorts, a rug, seven towels . . . it goes on and on. And every time we start a load of laundry we'd gather around in prayer, going, please, oh please, don't give us the error, please, just this time, please—ERROR, ERROR, ERROR.

Ten days later the repairman shows up to fix the machine because the part has been delivered, and oops! Guess he didn't order all the parts he needed! Going to have to order more parts! Another seven to ten days!

It takes a poet to tell compelling stories that include baby poop. Google "Maytag washer poor service" if you want to see the post; it's in the top four results.

As it turns out, Heather's sort of popular. Her book about mothering and postpartum depression,[2] *It Sucked and Then I Cried: How I Had a Baby, a Breakdown, and a Much Needed Margarita,* made the *New York Times* bestseller list in April of 2009. Her blog has a readership of about 350,000 unique visitors a month. Her readers are devoted; her posts tend to get a few hundred comments each. When it comes to moms, Heather has power.

Let's skip to the end here. Maytag's third visit to repair the machine failed. Heather called customer service. Back to the poetic rant:

I call the service department, explain in great detail what has happened, and she says that Maytag has a policy that they will not replace a brand new machine unless it is documented that someone has tried to fix it at least three times. WHA?? WHA-HAAA? And I tell her that someone has been out to my house three times, and she says, yeah, but he's only tried to fix it once . . .

Oh my Lord God IN HEAVEN. SHUT UP. You're kidding me, right? The three times he's been out here do not count? No. And the fact that this machine has not worked for two months? THAT doesn't count? No. And the fact that we bought the 10-yr-warranty? ALL OF THESE THINGS? DO YOU SEE THESE THINGS?

No.

So I call Maytag. The Maytag. The Mothership. And the agent I get after working through a five-minute maze of PRESS THIS and SAY THIS and PLEASE HOLD is the snootiest customer service person I have ever talked to in my life. And I let her know the entire story, front to back, and that while I'm really upset and sleep deprived, I'm not mad at her because I know it's not her fault. And she keeps saying, yeah, can't really help you, you're going to have to call and have the history faxed over, and then we'll take a look, and even then we'll schedule someone to come take a look, maybe in three to five days?

Okay then, I say, almost begging at this point, almost to the point of tears, is there anyone I can talk to who might see what I've been through and understand? And here's where I say, do you know what Twitter is? Because I have over a million followers on Twitter. If I say something about my terrible experience on Twitter do you think someone will help me? And she says in the most condescending tone and hiss ever uttered, "Yes, I know what Twitter is. And no, that will not matter."

Bad move, Maytag. Because now Heather starts tweeting. Her million-plus devoted followers on Twitter see this:

So that you may not have to suffer like we have: DO NOT EVER BUY A MAYTAG. I repeat: OUR MAYTAG EXPERIENCE HAS BEEN A NIGHTMARE.

Have I mentioned what a nightmare our experience was with Maytag? No? A TOTAL NIGHTMARE.

That brand new washing machine from MAYTAG? That someone has been out to fix three times? STILL BROKEN. DO NOT BUY MAYTAG.

Oh, also. I have a newborn. So we do, what, three loads of laundry a day? Except, our brand new washing machine IS BROKEN. DO NOT BUY MAYTAG.

Now Whirlpool (Maytag's parent company) will tell you this story has a happy ending. Whirlpool monitors social media; they see the tweets.[3] Unable to contact her by phone, they tweet back from their (admittedly seldom used) @WhirlpoolCorp account. Heather sends her phone number, and Whirlpool calls her the next morning. A more competent repair person comes and fixes the machine. And after two months of a Maytag that couldn't be depended on, and three weeks of abuse from service people, Heather's laundry emergency abates.

But the damage has been done. A million people have seen the tweets; how many have written off Maytag forever? Heather will not retract her rant; it's true, after all, and as she told us, "No one should have to go through this."

Her original blog post attracts 2,906 comments. *Forbes* writes a story about it.[4]

Whirlpool says it learned from what happened. Now it responds to tweets like this in public, on Twitter. That may make a difference in the future. But for now, it's clear that in a contest between a poetic blogger with a twelve-week-old and a 67,000-employee, $17-billion multinational company, there's no contest. The blogger won.

unleash your employees

Here's what you can learn from the parable of Maytag.

Individuals like Heather now have incredible amounts of power over companies. And not only through social technologies like blogs. With their smartphones they can connect from anywhere, anytime. They've got video. They've got Google, Facebook, and a thousand Internet start-ups empowering them.

Your company is not and cannot be nimble enough to serve them. With your established processes and departmental boundaries, you move too slowly.

Only your employees can help. And only if you unleash them.

The same technologies that empower your customers are available to your employees. Right now, they're using Facebook, YouTube, and Wikipedia and getting ideas about how to help your business. Technology is cheap and easy now. In marketing, in sales, and yes, in customer support, your staff are not just interested in reaching out to customers. In fact, they're ready to build solutions, applications, and systems that will transform your business. The question is: will you let them? You must, and here's why:

To succeed with empowered customers, you must empower your employees to solve customer problems.

This is much harder than it sounds. It means your staff are going to be coming up with solutions on their own. The ideas don't come from management; management's new job is to support and empower employees. The technology doesn't come from the information technology department; IT's new job is to support and encourage employees. It's a complete inversion of the top-down way companies run. And it's the only way to thrive in the age of the empowered customer.

Before you decide this is impossible, we'd like to show you a real, large, successful company where it's working: the electronics retailer Best Buy. The Best Buy story sounds a lot like the Maytag story, but the difference is in the empowered employees and what they do for the business.

CASE STUDY

Best Buy empowers its workforce

Josh Korin is a recruiter—his job is to help companies hire people. Like thousands of other people, he bought an Apple iPhone at Best Buy in February 2009. Because Josh doesn't like downtime, he also bought Best Buy's $14.99-a-month Geek Squad Black Tie product protection plan.

When the iPhone conked out six months after he bought it, he was annoyed of course, but he also felt pretty smart for buying that protection plan. That is, until he went back to the local Best Buy store, where they offered him a BlackBerry as a loaner until the iPhone was fixed. Josh reread the protection plan agreement and decided what he was owed was another iPhone, not a substitute. The manager at the Best Buy wouldn't budge, though. So Josh began to exercise his voice as an empowered individual.

As soon as he got home on August 29, Josh Korin's 596 Twitter followers saw dozens of messages from a very angry man. Here are a few. (The "@username" messages here are directed at a particular Twitter member, while the # indicates a "hashtag" included to make tweets show up in searches on that term.)

> Worst #customerservice ever? @bestbuy!! What's the point of Geek Squad phone insurance, if you replace an iPhone with a blackberry?

> #geeksquad whats the deal with your iPhone protection plan? replace an iPhone with a BlackBerry, WTF?! @bestbuy honor your insurance plan!

> @abril_dione do you have contact info for the CEO of #BestBuy? i am having a major customer service issue and I need to take it to the top!

> @bestbuycmo can you please help me resolve #bestbuy customer service issue? Iphone died, have insurance wont replace/honor protection plan!

Despite these complaints, this did not blow up into a PR nightmare like Maytag's. Hemmed in on one side by Amazon and on the other by Wal-Mart, Best Buy can't sell electronics as just a commodity; service is its major differentiator. So the company has invested in service, including monitoring people with problems on Twitter—searching continuously for tweets that mention terms like bestbuy and geeksquad.

Even though Josh was tweeting his complaints on a Saturday, two things happened right away. One was that Best Buy's CMO, Barry Judge—one of the main supporters of Best Buy's Twitter response force—responded from his own Twitter account at @bestbuycmo. He saw Josh's tweet since it mentioned his Twitter user name.

And second, Coral Biegler stepped in. Coral is a "community connector"—her job is to monitor Facebook, Twitter, blogs, and other forms of social communication for problems just like this. And she (@coral_bestbuy) immediately responded with this message:

> @joshkorin I understand this is frustrating, thanks for patience . . .
> I will be in office tomorrow to research & respond #twelpforce

This message is directed to Josh, but the tag "#twelpforce" indicates that it comes from Best Buy's Twitter Help Force. The Twelpforce includes both dedicated employees like Coral and members of Best Buy's blue-shirted floor sales team and Geek Squad service representatives. If you include "#twelpforce" in your tweets, any one of twenty-five hundred Best Buy employees who have signed up with Twelpforce could respond and try to help you out. They do it over a hundred times every day. (Check it out: go to http://twitter.com/twelpforce and you'll see all the responses.)

Of course, Twelpforce didn't just spontaneously spring into being. Two of the social technology veterans at Best Buy, Gary Koelling and Steve Bendt, helped conceive it with support and encouragement from Barry Judge. A technology wiz in the eCommerce group, Ben Hedrington, invented the technology. A marketing guy, John Bernier, found a way past obstacles including labor laws, legal problems, and technical challenges to make it work. Without John Bernier's ingenuity and perseverance, Coral Biegler would never have been in the position to respond, and Josh Korin would have been doing for Best Buy what Heather Armstrong did for Maytag—trashing it. What John Bernier and his team did—what they were permitted and empowered to do for Best Buy—is what really transformed this situation. They put Coral in a position to solve a customer's problem.

Coral called Josh Korin at home the next day, a Sunday. She arranged for him to go down to the store and get a loaner until his phone was fixed. "Coral was unbelievable," Josh told us. "She consistently said, 'I will find you a resolution, since you walked out of the store not satisfied, and that's not OK.'"

But this isn't the end of the story. Of course Josh is a loyal customer of Best Buy, now. Of course he tweeted that he's happy, and helped Best Buy to avoid its own Maytag moment. But what Coral didn't know at the time is that Josh's wife is @interactiveAmy, a Twitter member with over three thousand followers who gives presentations at places like the Social Media Breakfast group of Chicago (#smbchicago). Here's what interactiveAmy's Twitter followers were hearing:

> @coral_bestbuy just told the story of how u & @twelpforce helped @joshkorin to #smbchicago, they were so impressed!! Great job #bestbuy!

Josh Korin and his well-connected wife never got to create an avalanche of negative word of mouth for Best Buy, because Best Buy, with some timely, well-placed intervention, turned these detractors into promoters.

the HERO-powered business

We've got a word for people like Coral Biegler, John Bernier, and the rest of the people at Best Buy—and in companies all over the world—who are taking technology into their own hands and creating solutions for customer problems. They are highly empowered and resourceful operatives: HEROes for short.

Coral Biegler is a HERO in customer service. Twelpforce is a HERO brigade. John Bernier was the HERO who helped make it possible. None of these people is an IT professional, but all of them are comfortable using technology to solve customer problems. They're empowered and resourceful because Best Buy is run in such a way that they *can* be. It's a HERO-powered business.

When we published *Groundswell* in 2008, the challenge was creating strategies for connecting with customers in social environments like Facebook or blogs. As more and more companies do this, the challenge has shifted. The problem is not just connecting with empowered customers, it's what this engagement does to corporations. It's a *management* challenge. Because these technology projects are grassroots solutions conceived by HEROes, not top-down management initiatives, they require a transformation in the way companies operate.

The purpose of this book is to provide you with the tools to tackle this management challenge, to create and participate in a company that is HERO-powered. We'll explain how marketing, sales, customer service, management, and IT all need to change what they do and how they do it.

To lay the groundwork for this transformation, we'll start with a closer look at the technologies themselves—how they've grown, how they empower customers, and how HEROes can use them to solve customer problems.

the new groundswell

The shift toward empowered consumers affects every business now, whether you're selling washing machines, electronics, business services, banking, or entertainment; whether you're in Salt Lake City, Chicago, Mumbai, or Madrid.

We are all in information businesses now. Media isn't about books or DVDs, and financial services aren't about stocks—they're about information. Even for a manufactured product like a washing machine, the information about what it can do, whether it's any good, and where to find the best deal is central to the transaction. The information economy *is* the economy, since information surrounds every product, real or virtual.

Companies that made their money from having better information than their customers are now out of luck. It used to be that advertising determined the opening weekend gross of a movie, but when Sacha Baron Cohen's *Brüno* came out, ticket sales on the first weekend were already dropping on Saturday and Sunday,[5] because bad buzz spreads faster than advertising. If your product breaks after the first week, or your price is out of line, or you're offering coupons only in the store (or if your service puts parents of newborns through hell), your advantage is gone; everybody who counts will know within minutes. P. T. Barnum knew "there's a sucker born every minute," but now they won't stay suckers for long, because they have access to the information you're withholding.

The technologies behind this trend have grown and become more diverse. Four technologies now put more power in the hands of both customers and employees:

- *Smart mobile devices* extend connected experiences everywhere, independent of location, pushing the power of connections and better information into every crevice of your day.

- *Pervasive video,* created by both consumers and companies, has made the Internet into a full-on media experience.

- *Cloud computing services* mean that any connected device can access information and computing power embedded in the fabric of the Internet.

- *Social technology* has exploded—more than ever, people can influence and draw power from their peers, whether those peers are fellow customers or fellow employees.

These trends, taken together, are what we call the new groundswell. They reinforce one another, but always in the direction of the individual, whether in the marketplace or the workplace. While they give power to customers, they also create new opportunities to serve customers, and new ways for workers to connect with one another (see table 1-1). As we said, if you want to succeed with empowered customers, you must empower your employees to solve their problems. Now we'll show how this works for each of the component technologies.

smart mobile devices mean information is available everywhere

Three out of four consumers in America and four out of five in Western Europe have a mobile phone.[6] But don't think about phone calls. Think about phones as mobile information conduits. By 2009, 17 percent of the adult population, both in the United States and in Western Europe, already had mobile Internet service.[7] Every consumer with one of these phones is empowered with information and social connections, wherever they are.

For example, Occipital's $1.99 RedLaser iPhone app scans any bar code and tells you where the product is available online and what it

TABLE 1-1

The forces in the groundswell power shift apply in the marketplace and the workplace

Groundswell technology trend	How customers are empowered by it	How to serve customers with it	How workers benefit from it
Smart mobile devices	Get information about products and share it regardless of location (e.g., RedLaser iPhone app)	Create mobile applications to provide information to customers (e.g., E*TRADE Mobile Pro on smartphones)	Collaborate with colleagues and partners from any location (e.g., business email on BlackBerry)
Pervasive video	Cheaply create video commentary about companies; quickly see and spread user-generated video (e.g., "United Breaks Guitars" on YouTube)	Use video to inform or educate customers (e.g., author videos on Amazon.com, how-to videos on YouTube)	Improve training with video for visual learning (e.g., sales training videos by/for Black & Decker sales staff)
Cloud computing services	Get access to product information from thousands of cheap-to-get-going start-ups (e.g., real estate prices from zillow.com)	Inexpensively create online customer services (e.g., Bing maps on Hyatt.com)	Rapidly roll out and use collaboration applications (e.g., LotusLive.com for partner collaboration, Yammer for internal communication)
Social technology	Tap community for product information and to spread influence (e.g., ratings on Yelp)	Provide outreach to customers through online social applications (e.g., American Express "Open" community)	Build social applications to marshal employee innovations (e.g., idea-sharing applications for workers at Intuit, expertise location at Sogeti)

costs. Go ahead, use it in the supermarket or the bookstore. People armed with powerful mobile devices have more information power than the marketers and retailers they do business with.

With one hundred thirty thousand iPhone apps as we write this and millions of mobile Web sites, corporations are reaching out to serve consumers through these same channels. E*TRADE's mobile applications have created loyalty with its fast-moving trader customers. And with so many employees now using BlackBerry phones, iPhones, and other smart mobile devices, companies are providing their employees with access to corporate information—not just email, but customer and product databases—on mobile devices as well. People need to collaborate wherever they are, not just at their desks but in meetings, at home, and on the road.

pervasive video transforms the online experience

The Web has been a text-and-graphics medium for most of its short history. Now video is taking its place at the center of many Web experiences. In one month in 2009, according to Comscore, 100 million Americans watched a total of 6 billion YouTube videos.[8] Cisco says that in 2008, video represented 21 percent of all the data flowing over the Internet, and estimates that will reach 91 percent by 2013.[9] More importantly, individuals now have access to inexpensive, reasonable-quality video tools, including sub-$150 video cameras from Flip (a Cisco subsidiary) and Kodak and mobile phones that shoot video now, too.

The result is that anything that happens anywhere is likely to be recorded and sometimes posted for all to see. Four hundred thousand people viewed a video of then–U.S. senator George Allen's use of the obscure racial epithet *macaca* to refer to a campaign worker;[10] partly because of this remark, he's not a senator any more. Anything your employees do, anywhere, is about to be public in a very visual way.

If customers want videos, companies will give it to them. The *Wall Street Journal*'s home page now features video news analysis every day; sites from Home Depot to Amazon share video tips on their sites. Even the Realize Gastric Band, a surgically implanted device for obesity treatment, has its own YouTube channel.[11]

Cisco also pushes those Flip video cameras for internal sharing within corporations, and it's working; more and more people are communicating with video. Salespeople in particular seem to be open to visual learning through video.

cloud computing services aggregate power to benefit individuals

Online sites and services come from servers embedded in the Internet cloud. Online hosting services including Amazon's EC2, Google's App

Engine, and Microsoft's Azure make it easy for entrepreneurs to launch new information services for next to nothing. Developers can test and build applications that empower consumers with no more investment than a few thousand dollars. Zillow.com will tell you how much your house is worth, based on recent sales of comparable houses. Farecast, now part of Microsoft's Bing search engine, monitors airline prices and predicts whether they will go up or down. When computing power is cheap and information can be gathered online, there's no barrier to some bright developer building a service around it.

The same cloud computing resources that empower consumers make it possible for companies—or individuals within them—to reach out quickly. Any corporate site can embed a map from Google or Bing. When Derek Gottfrid needed raw computing power to process terabytes of digitized images for the *New York Times*'s "Times Machine" archive, he just rented computing time on Amazon's EC2 servers—for several hundred dollars.[12] The *New York Times* hosts TimesMachine.com on Amazon's servers, too, and pays only for the resources used.

More and more, corporate applications are running in the cloud as well. Corporate service providers like Salesforce.com (customer relationship management), Yammer (internal messaging), and Socialtext (knowledge sharing) aren't software, they're cloud Internet services accessible with a login from any Internet-connected device. When the servers, software, and storage are in the cloud, workers can use these services efficiently from any connected device.

social technologies have become universal

In the United States at the end of 2009, 59 percent of all online consumers were in social networks[13]; Facebook now has over 400 million members. In some places, like South Korea, three out of four online consumers connect with social content at least once a month.[14] The result of all this is that you can tap into your friends—or strangers—for help with anything. Buying a DVD? The reviews on IMDb (Internet Movie Database) will tell you if it's a cult hit or a dog. Whether a company's product is a lemon, a retailer is charging a higher price than others, or a supplier delivers poor service, the information is instantly available.

Corporate social applications have taken off. Nearly every technology company has a support forum where customers help each other solve technical problems. Companies from Ford to Coca-Cola use Facebook, Twitter, and blogs—both their own and their fans'—to spread the word about their products.

Internally, social technologies connect workers. At the Spanish megabank BBVA, workers share in an internal blogosphere. At the airline information supplier Sabre, employees communicate on a Facebook-style internal social network called cubeless. Companies from Dell and Intuit to the insurance giant Chubb are using social applications to surface and support innovations that their employees come up with. Workers say they benefit from these connections every bit as much as consumers do.

build a HERO-powered business

All these technologies are immediately accessible. All are free or cheap for customers. All are accessible to employee HEROes. The tools to change your business, to become more responsive to these empowered consumers, aren't the problem. It's the way your business runs that needs to change.

In the first half of this book, we describe what HEROes actually do. We show you the full range of HERO projects and provide you with tools to evaluate whether the value of such a project is worth the effort. We follow this with a detailed survey-based analysis of different types of empowered customers and introduce the four-step process your company needs to square up to them, which we call IDEA: *identify* mass influencers, *deliver* groundswell customer service, *empower* customers with mobile information, and *amplify* the voice of your fans.

In the second half of the book, we describe how management and technology work in concert to create a HERO-powered business. Managing a business like this means setting up technology and management structures and creating a culture that grants a lot more autonomy to the employee problem solvers—a challenge both for top-down managers and locked-down information technology departments. We start this discussion by addressing the HERO Compact—the deal your

HEROes, your management, and your IT group must make so that people can generate solutions, not just chaos. We'll show you the patterns in employee use of technology and how to manage them. We also discuss how IT and managers can boost the power of HEROes with systems that encourage innovation and collaboration. Finally, we'll describe how IT can not only support employees with technology, but keep their companies safe and secure as well.

Harnessing the power of HEROes is a difficult journey for most companies, but it's worth it. At the end you will be not just more customer focused, but also more collaborative and agile. When you see what the HEROes in our book have done for their companies, we think you'll see it's a journey worth taking.

what HEROes do

2. employee HEROes
and their projects

Rob Sharpe is a do-it-yourself kind of guy. He likes to build stuff; he remodeled his own kitchen and built a deck on his house. So it's no surprise that he's a loyal fifteen-year veteran employee of Black & Decker,[1] a company that makes power tools. And it's no surprise that when it came time to improve the way Black & Decker trains its sales staff, Rob Sharpe figured out a perfect do-it-yourselfer's solution.

Rob is head of sales training, which is a big deal at Black & Decker. The company has hundreds of complex products, which have to be explained and sold to retailers as huge as Home Depot and as small as your local mom-and-pop hardware store, so they in turn can serve up the information to consumers. And Black & Decker has lots of competition. Whether it's a reciprocating saw from Makita or a cordless power screwdriver from Hitachi, Black & Decker's sales staff need to know just how their tools stack up—a task that, as you might imagine, is always changing.

Black & Decker's sales training appeared to be doing just fine, with an in-house learning system that organized the documents and Power-Point slides. Rob and his team would bring the sales folks in and run them through training in a 17,000-square-foot workshop outside Baltimore, Maryland, with every imaginable device for working with wood, tile, screws, nails, and concrete. But Rob had an inkling there was a better way.

In 2007, Rob got a close look at YouTube. Where others saw cats on skateboards and bad music video takeoffs, he saw potential. Then, about a year later, he got a look at the Flip video camera, a $150 device about the size of a pack of cigarettes, and brain-dead-simple to operate. "I'm a visual learner," thought Rob. "A lot of these tool guys are visual learners." So he got the idea to include video in the Black & Decker sales training. Consumers use YouTube for fun; why shouldn't he use the same technique for training?

But because Rob is a highly empowered and resourceful operative, he took the video idea one step further. First, he worked with his reluctant IT group to set up a video server, so he would have space to upload a lot more videos. "The initial resistance from IT," he says, "was not really about the project, but about security and getting space on the server." Rob talked them into it.

And second, he started arming the do-it-yourself sales staff with the tools to make their own videos. "Why wouldn't I issue a Flip camera to everyone who goes through a presentation skills course?" asks Rob. They're so cheap, after all. He also equipped the staff with Windows Moviemaker, a simple, free video-editing program, and showed them how to use it.

Then an amazing thing happened. The do-it-yourselfers started creating their own training materials.

One guy started sending in video of competitors' products, highlighting their weaknesses in a highly visual way that other salespeople could really relate to. Rob calls this video the "seed" since once other salespeople saw it, they immediately saw the value of video. And they saw they could create it easily, too.

More video started pouring in. Salespeople began documenting their challenges, their product features, and the solutions that worked best in sales situations. "Now we get fifteen to twenty videos a month," he says, and you can tell he's excited to have created something so useful. "How power tools are used on job sites. Feedback on the tools. And the content is already completely edited"—that is, ready for viewing.

Rob was able to succeed because his boss, Les Ireland, Black & Decker's president of commercial operations in North America, supported his efforts. As Les puts it, "The concept of getting our teams involved in delivering 'real world' content was a powerful idea." Like any good manager, he weighs these decisions carefully. "How quickly can we execute a new technology in order to capture the productivity across our commercial team is always a critical question," he says. The emphasis on speed here is what sets apart the best managers of HEROes—they look not just for benefits, but for benefits delivered quickly.

Rob's team used to spend hours building PowerPoint training courses. Now he and his staff review videos, upload them, and highlight what's most useful. And he makes his own videos. "I will not let people in this department create a forty-five-minute course again," he says. "It's not what the staff need or what they want. Speed to execution is just as important. The training staff can spend a half hour with the product, come up with our own opinions and competitive analysis, and send it out the next day with an assessment."

Now videos on the Black & Decker server can attract hundreds of views from Black & Decker workers; the most popular videos get viewed by over half of the sales force. Training that used to take two weeks now takes one. New staff spend fifteen hours online before even coming to the training center. Senior management, corporate marketing, and public relations people are perusing the training site for useful bits of content and motivational nuggets.

And in the ultimate turnaround, the IT group is now using the same video techniques to train people on stuff like how to set up 3G mobile broadband in laptops.

Rob turned the tools that consumers use into visual training. Why? Because he's a tool guy and a do-it-yourselfer, a highly empowered and resourceful HERO. It just made sense to him. And eventually, once he got it working, to the whole sales and management team at Black & Decker.

HEROes and their projects are diverse

At your company, what happens to people like Rob? If you were Rob's boss, would you support and encourage his experiment? Or would you shut it down, tell him to go back and do his job of creating PowerPoints, and avoid the hassle of trying to lobby people in IT and marketing?

If you're like most managers, you'd probably respond, "It depends."

Empowering your workforce means saying yes to HEROes more often. It also means saying no to projects where the effort, budget, or risk is too great, or where the value is questionable. Some of the projects connect directly with customers (like Best Buy's Twelpforce) and others, like Rob's video sharing, help employees in customer-facing departments like sales, but they all need a careful evaluation of effort versus value.

We've now reviewed dozens of HERO projects like Rob's. Here's what managers need to know about the people who come up with these projects: they're doers, like Rob Sharpe. They're not rebels. They want to help the organizations they work for to be successful; they're often the most enthusiastic backers of the companies' goals and missions. But they're also driven by a desire to create improvements on their own initiative, rather than to live with the status quo.

What varies is the size of their projects, their level of technical skill, and their roles in the company. What's constant is their natural desire to take up the new technologies that now surround us all—mobile, video, cloud, and social—to create solutions.

For example, Mark Betka, a program officer in the U.S. State Department, wanted to get positive messages about America out to people all around the world. He came up with the idea of creating international teleconferences between prominent Americans and ordinary citizens in other countries. Unwilling to be stopped by a lack of funding, Mark found an unused license for Adobe Connect—a cloud Internet service for online meetings and videoconferences—and created "CO.NX: A Public Diplomacy Outreach Project" pretty much on his own. Among many other events, CO.NX hosted sessions that included a marketing expert in Hartford, Connecticut, training Iraqi widows on how to market their crafts internationally on the Web and thousands of people commenting live on President Barack Obama's address in Ghana. Mark used Facebook to promote the program. The CO.NX Facebook page[2] has ninety thousand fans and lists several programs a week, some of which get audiences in the tens of thousands.

Molly Mattessich had a little bit bigger project in mind. She's manager of online initiatives at the National Peace Corps Association, a nonprofit group that advocates for the overseas efforts of the U.S. Peace

Corps and connects and supports former Peace Corps workers when they return home. In "forty days and forty nights," as she puts it (actually, it took a few months), she hired developers to create an online community called Africa Rural Connect,[3] uniting former Peace Corps workers and Africans living around the world to find new ways to help African farmers succeed. Within months, twelve thousand people from one hundred eighty countries had created profiles and contributed almost eight hundred ideas for a contest to reward the best rural farming ideas.

Some HEROes take on projects that could just as easily be major IT efforts. Take Boyd Beasley, who runs most of customer support at the game company Electronic Arts. He developed a system that allows the company's game-playing customers to contact support from right in the middle of the game. As a result, people having some sort of technical challenge while in the middle of a quest or contest don't have to quit the game or make a call. Using offshore developers in India, he designed a system that hooks the game directly into the interfaces for his support function. Even though this project cost half a million dollars to implement, customer support had to run it; the IT and game development resources are all focused on game-play features, not technical support.

These projects are all over the map. Some were simple, some were complex. But what they all had in common was a clear expectation that the value being created was in line with the effort required.

sizing up HERO projects

HERO projects vary widely in size, scope, and benefits to the company. But all these projects generate resistance. As we explain throughout this book, ideally management, IT, and HEROes in customer-facing departments work together. But in a typical company today, HEROes face challenges from all over the organization: senior management, the legal department, and IT people. Sometimes the value the HERO is attempting to create makes the effort worth it. Sometimes it's not.

To help managers to evaluate these decisions, we've created a tool called the EVE Score (EVE stands for Effort-Value Evaluation). Before starting (or supporting) a project, you should answer the questions in this evaluation to see what you're in for (see tables 2-1 and 2-2).

TABLE 2-1

Effort questions

1. Tools: Does the project require tools or resources? (Select all that apply.)

   a. Requires a purchase from a software or service vendor: Add 5 points

   b. Requires IT involvement for access to applications: Add 5 points

   c. Requires IT involvement for security: Add 5 points

   d. Requires help from an outside development company: Add 5 points

   e. No additional tools required or tools are free: 0 points

2. Time: How long will the project likely take to show results? (Select one.)

   a. Less than 2 weeks: 0 points

   b. 2–8 weeks: 5 points

   c. 3–4 months: 10 points

   d. 5–6 months: 15 points

   e. More than 6 months: 20 points

3. Cost: What is the total budget? (Select one.)

   a. Less than $500: 0 points

   b. $500 to $2,000: 5 points

   c. $2,000 to $10,000: 10 points

   d. $10,000 to $50,000: 15 points

   e. More than $50,000: 20 points

4. People: How many people are involved in the development? (Select one.)

   a. Just the HERO: 0 points

   b. The HERO plus 1 other person: 5 points

   c. 3–5 people: 10 points

   d. 6–10 people: 15 points

   e. More than 10 people: 20 points

5. Governance: Does the project require any of the following? (Select all that apply.)

   a. Approval from the HERO's immediate boss: Add 0 points

   b. Legal or compliance approval: Add 5 points

   c. Security or risk management approval: Add 5 points

   d. Accounting or finance approval: Add 5 points

   e. Public relations approval—project affects corporate image: Add 5 points

   f. IT group approval: Add 5 points

   g. No approval necessary: Add 0 points

Add the answers to effort questions 1 through 5 to create the effort score.

TABLE 2-2

Value questions

1. Revenue: Does the project increase revenue? (Select all that apply.)
   a. Creates a new product or service customers can buy: Add 20 points
   b. Shortens the buying cycle by more than 10%: Add 10 points
   c. Increases the average order size by 10%: Add 10 points
   d. Makes company's products or services relevant for new customer groups: Add 10 points
   e. Increases revenue significantly in some other way: Add 10 points
   f. Does not increase revenue: Add 0 points

2. Cost: Does the project save money? (Select all that apply.)
   a. Decreases marketing costs: Add 20 points
   b. Decreases customer service costs: Add 20 points
   c. Decreases the cost of sales: Add 20 points
   d. Allows measurement (e.g., marketing effectiveness) that will lead to cost savings: Add 10 points
   e. Saves money in other measurable ways: Add 10 points
   f. Does not save money: Add 0 points

3. Productivity: Does the project make an internal process more efficient? (Select all that apply.)
   a. Improves internal communication: Add 10 points
   b. Improves the speed of resolving an issue: Add 10 points
   c. Improves the quality of an outcome: Add 10 points
   d. Streamlines or accelerates a process: Add 10 points
   e. Improves sales productivity: Add 10 points
   f. Improves another important business metric: Add 10 points
   g. Improves the effectiveness of 20 or more employees: Add 10 points
   h. Does not make an internal process more efficient: Add 0 points

4. Advocacy: Does the project improve loyalty and positive word of mouth? (Select all that apply.)
   a. Leads to higher customer satisfaction or improves customer loyalty: Add 10 points
   b. Improves the customer experience in some measurable way: Add 10 points
   c. Creates more influential word-of-mouth advocates: Add 10 points
   d. Has a track record of turning detractors into advocates: Add 15 points
   e. Does not improve loyalty and positive word of mouth: Add 0 points

5. Reach: Does the project increase the organization's reach? (Select all that apply.)
   a. Helps marketing messages to reach 20% more people: Add 10 points
   b. Helps marketing messages to reach better-qualified people: Add 10 points
   c. Generates between 10% and 20% more leads: Add 10 points
   d. Generates more than 20% more leads: Add 20 points
   e. Generates better-qualified leads: Add 10 points
   f. Increases brand awareness in at least one new geography or market: Add 10 points
   g. Does not increase the organization's reach: Add 0 points

Add the answers to value questions 1 through 5 to create the value score.

We've also put this evaluation online at http://www.forrester.com/empowered.

The EVE Score is intended to help you think through what you're about to do. The first set of questions, the effort questions, show where you'll encounter resistance, not just in gathering resources and budget, but in parts of the company that may need to be brought in, like IT, PR, or legal. The second set, the value questions, help to clarify the exact benefits you're seeking.

Based on these two scores, you can evaluate whether the project is worth it—whether the effort exceeds the value, or vice versa. Our evaluation can't capture all the challenges or all the sources of value, so you may want to go beyond the scores in your own assessment, but at least you'll have an idea of how to balance the two sides of the equation, effort and value.

Finally, you'll be able to evaluate your project in context, to determine just how big a task you're taking on. Boyd Beasley's in-game support system was a huge job. Molly Mattessich's online community was much more manageable. You want to go into these projects with a clear idea of which size project you'll be working on.

the six types of projects and what to do about them

Based on your scores for value and effort, you'll end up in one of six categories (see figure 2-1). The first two are cases where the value and effort are out of alignment, the no-brainer and the Quixote project.

- *No-brainer (value exceeds effort by more than 25 points).* If the value score exceeds the effort by this much, what's stopping you? It's a surprise you're not funded already. These projects don't really require a HERO, they're part of the way everyone does business, like maintaining a simple Web page to update customers on information.

- *Quixotic quagmire (effort exceeds value by more than 25 points).* If your effort is this much out of line with the value, you're probably making a big mistake. (It's also possible that there's some major source of value that's not captured in our evaluation,

FIGURE 2-1

Projects fall into one of six categories

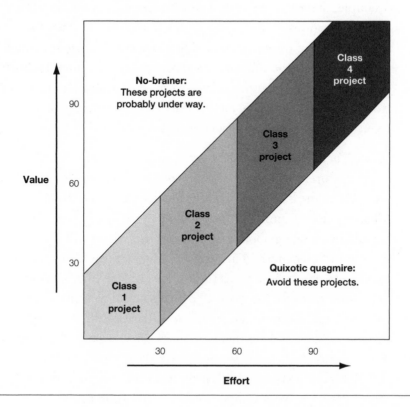

but you'd better make certain of that before proceeding.) Still, the impulse to create this project had to come from somewhere. HEROes and their managers in this category should work to find ways to increase the value or decrease the effort. Or table the project until conditions improve—for example, new technologies may make the project more viable in the future than it is now.

If your value and effort scores are within 25 points of one another, you've got a viable project where value and effort are commensurate. But you need to know what you're in for. Viable projects fall into four classes based on the level of effort required.

- *Class 1, or simple fix (effort less than 30).* With a score this low, the HERO is just doing her job with a little more creativity. For example, she might be using a spreadsheet to tally up sales from different regions, or reviewing Web site statistics to track the effectiveness of different marketing programs. Managers should routinely encourage this sort of activity to stimulate more HERO-type thinking in the future. If these projects are a major challenge, you're working for a very locked-down company; creative managers may want to go somewhere else.

- *Class 2, or cool idea (effort 30 or more, but less than 60).* A little higher effort score means you're involved with something more valuable to the business, but more challenging—like Rob Sharpe's video training project or Best Buy's Twelpforce. You should be thinking about two things. First, where will you encounter resistance? Managers should review the effort scores to see whom you need to recruit to help, as Rob Sharpe did to get server space for his videos. You'll also want to think about whether legal, accounting, regulatory affairs, or PR staff will have a problem and get them on board early, because these are groups who react poorly to surprises and can shut you down. HEROes and managers with projects in this category need to do a little homework to have a value justification ready.

- *Class 3, or major project (effort 60 or more, but less than 90).* Effort scores of 60 or higher mean you've got a big job on your hands. It's likely your project will touch multiple departments, need to hire outside resources, or take quite a while to complete. Molly Mattessich's Africa Rural Connect community is an example. You'll need to do all the tasks we recommended for Class 2 projects, but you should also expect to spend more of your time on politics. For these sorts of projects, you'll need a more precise justification on the value side, with estimates of how your project will increase sales, reduce costs, increase efficiency, improve brand awareness, or the like. You'd better be good with a spreadsheet. A project of this class requires a conversation with the IT department, since you'll probably get in over your head unless you're a real technology wizard. As we describe later in the book, IT's role is changing; advising HEROes on these sorts of projects will become part of IT's job.

- *Class 4, or shadow IT (effort 90 or higher).* If your score exceeds 90, face it, you're doing stuff that used to be done by technology professionals within enterprises. Boyd Beasley's in-game support project is a good example of shadow IT. Why isn't IT doing these sorts of projects? Because of cutbacks in IT budgets, in many cases they end up being paid for by customer-facing departments like marketing, sales, and support. Shadow IT has a bad name among IT professionals, and for good reason—many of these large, ongoing efforts go awry, leaving people in over their heads from a budgetary perspective, facing technical problems they can't figure out, or messing up other corporate technology efforts. This doesn't mean you shouldn't undertake a project like this. But to move forward, you'll need to collaborate with senior management and IT to increase the likelihood of success. You may also need help from an experienced system integrator or developer like IBM, Sapient, or Razorfish.

Class 3 and 4 projects are significantly more complex and challenging. To see what it's like to complete one, we'll share the story of Ross Inglis, who undertook a shadow-IT-level project to create a new set of customers for Thomson Reuters.

CASE STUDY

Thomson Reuters finds new customers in the cloud

Thomson Reuters collects real-time financial data, descriptions, lists of executives, and other crucial information about nearly every decent-sized company on the planet. If you want to know about a company, stop first at Thomson Reuters—you'll be smarter. It's a perfect example of the kind of information that empowers customers.

Ross Inglis is responsible for, among other things, alliances and distribution partners in the Americas. So he's continually trying to find new markets for Thomson Reuters's information. In 2007, he began to see an opportunity for the company, one that would come from an untapped market—independent investment advisors—and a new way to distribute content, through the cloud.

First, the market. There are nearly half a million independent investment advisors in the United States. They typically have dozens or hundreds of clients—but not thousands. They're very interested in company information, since quick access can help them make investment recommendations. But unlike Thomson's current customers, they're not large institutions willing to pay six- or seven-figure fees and install infrastructure to get access to information. A hundred bucks a month is a serious expense for these folks. Not only that, they need a solution that's easy to install and trouble free to use.

That's where the Internet cloud comes in. Cloud services are lightweight and easy to deploy, just what investment advisors need. They scale up without any capital investment. And in this case, there's a natural channel. Salesforce.com's contact management system is attractive to small firms like investment advisors exactly because it's cloud based: you just hook up to the Internet and point your browser at a site, and all your contacts are instantly available. Salesforce.com is so connected to the cloud, its logo is actually the word *software* with a circle and slash—"no software"—to indicate that there's nothing to install. If Thomson could piggyback its information onto Salesforce.com's contact management tool, the result would be just right for investment advisors—easy to get to through a browser, and with both contact information and corporate data available just when the advisors needed it.

So in late 2007, Ross set out to build a product to deliver Thomson Reuters's information through Salesforce.com.

This application started, as many do, with unstructured exploration. One of Ross's staffers was an application developer; Ross pointed him at Salesforce.com and asked him to try it out. This was followed, as Ross puts it, by a period of "playing around." As with many HERO projects, exploration without a detailed goal is often required to get a feel for what's actually possible. Play is fine, as long as you don't make a long-term career out of it.

Next, Ross lined up a senior sponsor, a necessary step for a project of this size—one that will go on for many months, chew up tens of thousands of dollars in budget, and eventually make an impression on customers. Ross's manager, Matthew Burkley, gave him free rein because he recognized the size of the opportunity. Salesforce had just signed major deals with Merrill Lynch and Citibank, so clearly it was a distribution channel worth pursuing.

The next step was prototyping. Prototyping on a Class 4 project is an excellent idea, because you'll probably have to line up a bunch of internal stakeholders, many of whom will feel the need to see what you're planning for themselves. Ross hired a firm that has since become a division of Fujitsu to build his prototype and show how customers would benefit.

As a project of this nature goes forward, the HERO finds that his most heroic qualities are political, not technical. Ross explains that this project "took a lot of persuasion and cajoling and bartering. Apparently I'm good at that," he adds, not too modestly. "I am able to get what I want. People I need support from become sick of hearing from me, or find I can help them in other ways."

One essential political element to negotiate in a large project is the support of the technology department. In Ross's case this meant checking with two different CTOs during the course of the project. Working with these CTOs accomplished two things. It surfaced important technical issues, like data security, that the project needed to address to become a key distribution channel for the company. And it kept the IT department from blocking the project later due to unaddressed concerns or politics. While Ross didn't do everything the CTOs suggested—some of it was just too expensive—he was able to include them in his list of allies as the project moved forward.

At this writing the project is on schedule. Ross has hired some Uruguayan developers recommended by Salesforce.com and expects the product to roll out and start producing over a million dollars in business in 2010. And it will come in for a total development budget of $100,000.

Ross has also accomplished some of his personal goals. His visibility in the organization has risen. People from other parts of the company come to him for advice. He's also upset some people by pursuing a project that extends beyond his normal job description, and by inventing new ways of doing business that upset the status quo. But thanks to his heroic political skills, those skeptics won't keep his project from getting its chance to succeed and make money for Thomson Reuters.

a few words for HEROes

From the examples of Black & Decker and Thomson Reuters, you can see what it takes to be an employee HERO. While most of this book concentrates on managers and what they need to do, it helps to understand the HERO's challenge. So we'll leave you with a few words of advice for HEROes.

First, focus on customers. The closer you get to making customers more empowered and happier, the easier it will be to justify your project. Helping people who touch customers—like salespeople and support people—is also a good idea. But when you're calculating the impact of your project, it's customer value that will keep you going.

Second, most HERO projects are based on better flow of information. Consider new forms of communication, like Rob Sharpe's salesperson videos, or new ways to put customers in touch with their information, like Ross Inglis's financial advisor product. But if you improve information to empower customers or customer-facing staff, you're probably on the right track.

Third, assess both your level of effort and the value you'll be producing. Why? It's not just to know how big a project you're taking on. The value questions will help clarify the ways you can prove your project is worth it, while the effort questions will help you identify where the challenges are. You'll be able to see whether you need to concentrate on raising budgetary support, making information technology decisions that don't run afoul of IT, or winning over line-of-business managers. Without this sort of planning, you'll doubtless run into unanticipated trouble, and it's your own fault—you should have thought through who and what could get in your way before you started.

Fourth, it's harder than you think. HEROes are always going off the beaten track. HEROes learn about groundswell technologies and want to harness them, but rarely realize just how disruptive they may be to organizations. What looks easy turns out to be hard. What looks hard may be even harder than you thought. We tell you this, not to scare you, but to encourage you to prepare for adversity—political, technical, and personal—because that's what completing a HERO project nearly always means.

Finally, don't stop with one HERO project. Your project will raise your visibility, as well as tease your customers and fellow staff with new ideas about what's possible. The rewards of success are higher demands. Think about what you're going to do about those demands, and how you will maintain and improve what you've built.

what HEROes do

The job of a HERO is to find ways to boost the business by connecting with empowered customers. In the next four chapters, we'll describe exactly how to do that in four steps that we call the IDEA process: identify empowered customers, deliver groundswell customer service, empower them further with mobile information, and amplify their word of mouth.

3. peer influence analysis

Stop me if you've heard this one.

A guy walks onto a plane in Halifax, Nova Scotia, in the spring of 2008. He's a musician starting a tour through Nebraska. He checks his guitar.

Later that day, as he's getting on the connecting flight in Chicago, he hears a woman say "My God, they're throwing guitars out there." And sure enough, the baggage handlers are heaving musical instruments around like sacks of potatoes.

By now, many of you have figured out that the guy is Dave Carroll and the airline is United. If you know the story, you know that Dave Carroll went from being a not-very-well-known local musician to being about as empowered as one guy can get.

The base of Dave's $3,500 Taylor guitar was smashed.[1] United's baggage claims agents refused to pay the $1,200 cost of the repair, citing a policy about the timeframe in which claims need to be filed. So he took things into his own hands. He wrote a song called "United Breaks Guitars," spent $150 to make a video for it with his band, and loaded the video onto YouTube in July of 2009.[2] It's a pretty catchy tune, and of course, the video features (dramatized) careless baggage handlers. By that night, twenty-five thousand people had seen it. The Halifax *Herald* covered it. The *Los Angeles Times* covered it. So did CNN.

Since then, more than 7 million people have viewed it.

Here's what life has been like for Dave Carroll since then. He's been interviewed in the news media two hundred fifty times. He's schmoozed with Whoopi Goldberg on *The View*.[3] His Web site is getting fifty thousand hits a day. His CDs are selling like mad. CTV, the largest private broadcaster in Canada, hired him as a songwriter. He's got an endorsement deal with Carlton, a company that makes hard guitar cases. And he's getting a different kind of gig now—companies are hiring him as a social media expert.

Meanwhile, United Airlines is doing penance for the insensitivity of its baggage handlers and claims agents. Sysomos, a company that monitors online mentions of companies, including sentiment (positive or negative), tracked a spike in social chatter about United Airlines just after "United Breaks Guitars" went live, especially on Twitter.[4] Examining sentiment in blogs in the hundreds of posts mentioning United in the quarters before and after the incident, positive sentiment went down from 34 to 28 percent; negative increased from 22 to 25 percent. (The rest were neutral.) And the fallout in traditional media was worse—positive stories dropped from 39 to 27 percent, while negative stories increased from 18 to 23 percent. Six months after "United Breaks Guitars," requests to talk about it still were coming in to United PR almost daily.

United has changed its policies. Baggage claims agents now have a little more discretion with customers whose special situations warrant the company looking into the claim more closely; United uses Dave Carroll's video in its training. And the company has begun monitoring social media regularly, so it can respond to people and cut red tape before they get mad enough to broadcast their anger more publicly. But "United Breaks Guitars" continues to resonate, since it reinforces people's ideas about insensitive airlines. People will be talking about this for a long time to come.

was your last customer Dave Carroll?

Let's unpack what's really going on with United and Dave Carroll—or in any case where empowered customers disrupt a company.

In traditional marketing you send out messages to masses of people. You count those instances as "impressions." You hope your message, repeated frequently enough, impresses your audience. One ad campaign might create 7 million impressions.

Using the reach of YouTube, Dave Carroll created 7 million impressions by himself (and for $150—what's your TV ad budget?). The baggage handlers and claims agents were his unwitting collaborators. It's practically an ad campaign run by a single empowered customer.

Now we'll quantify this phenomenon. At Forrester, we surveyed ten thousand people at the end of 2009.[5] We asked about the environments in which they spread influence, like Facebook, Twitter, and blogs. Here's what we found.[6]

Within social networks, consumers create 256 billion impressions on one another by talking about products and services each year.[7]

In social environments like blogs and discussion forums and on sites that feature ratings and reviews, customers generate 1.64 billion posts.[8] While we can't know how many people view each post, based on data we've collected about readership of blogs and forums, we estimate that this content creates at least another 250 billion impressions. Combined with the social networks, that's more than half a trillion impressions in the United States. On average, that's about eight impressions every day on every person online.

Here's one way to look at the connections empowered consumers are making. According to Nielsen Online, advertisers delivered 1.974 trillion online ad impressions in the twelve months ending in September 2009, the time period covered by our survey.[9] Do the math. People receive roughly one-fourth as many impressions from *each other* as they do from online advertisers.

Which ones do you think they pay attention to?

Does your marketing budget reflect the reach of empowered customers? What are you doing to make it work for you? What are you doing to stop it from working *against* you?

a strategy IDEA for energizing your customers

The reason marketers generally haven't harnessed these empowered consumers is simple. They know how to use concepts like reach, positioning, and key performance indicators to design marketing strategy and measure effectiveness. But they have no plan of attack for word of mouth, and no vocabulary to talk about it.

The other problem is that marketers work with masses: mass media and mass impressions. Empowered customers are individuals. Marketers don't deal with individuals—customer service people do. Customer service is typically treated as a cost center, so service representatives serve customers as cheaply as possible. Unfortunately, that level of service is what creates the Dave Carrolls of the world.

Starting now, we want you to think about individuals as potential sources of marketing influence, either positive or negative. Your customer is a marketing channel. Every manager in a customer-facing department must therefore conceive of her job as to create more positive, and less negative, influence—and to do it as efficiently as possible. In *Groundswell*, we called this "energizing your customers." It's a new way to think about marketing, service, and customers.

How to do this? In a HERO-powered business, managers across all customer-facing departments need to connect with empowered customers. Here's the four-step game plan with the mnemonic IDEA:

- *Identify* the mass influencers. Concentrate on the people most likely to spread messages about your company.

- *Deliver* groundswell customer service. Reach out through groundswell channels and serve these vocal and influential customers.

- *Empower* your customers with information, especially mobile information. Keep people happy by surrounding them with the information they need.

- *Amplify* your fans. Find the people who love you, and boost the impact they have on their peers.

In this chapter, we'll concentrate on identifying mass influencers, but the rest is coming. Chapter 4 shows how to do groundswell customer service. Chapter 5 tells how to create mobile empowerment. And chapter 6 is your plan for fan marketing.

who are mass influencers?

In 2000, Malcolm Gladwell wrote an incredibly insightful book called *The Tipping Point*.[10] He identified three groups of people who help spread trends. The first is a group called Connectors, people who know a wide variety of other folks through some sort of social connection. He also identified a group he called Mavens, who know stuff—these are the experts on wine, on fashion, on cars—whatever. (His third group, the Salesmen, don't enter into the discussion in this chapter.)

Based on our research, these people have fascinating online analogs. Online Connectors are the people with lots of social network connections—people with a huge Twitter following, or a lot of Facebook friends, and who connect with their followers frequently. Online Mavens correspond to the people who post content online—they blog, or comment on blogs; they post in discussion forums; or they write reviews on sites like Amazon.com.

Using our survey, we examined these groups. We found out a few things that are very important for marketers and other customer-facing staffers to know. First of all, only a small subset of online connectors and online mavens accounts for nearly all of the influence; we call them mass influencers. And second, while mass influencers are a small percentage of the online consumers, there are still millions of them, so a one-person-at-a-time strategy isn't appropriate. Make no mistake: mass influencers are a channel. You can let them say whatever they want, as Dave Carroll did, and then react. Or you can work proactively to get them sharing messages in line with your strategy.

Mass influencers come in two flavors: the *Mass Connectors*, who have the most influence within social networks, and the *Mass Mavens*, who have the most influence in content channels like blogs and discussion forums.

Mass Connectors live in the moment and connect with their friends

Who are the influential people on social networks? When we set out to answer this question, we suspected some sort of 80-20 rule would

FIGURE 3-1

Mass Connectors account for 80 percent of the online influence in social networks

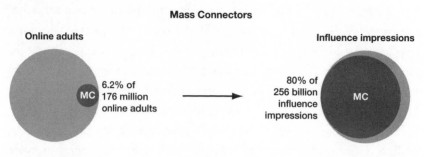

Mass Connectors

Online adults
Influence impressions

MC 6.2% of 176 million online adults

80% of 256 billion influence impressions
MC

Base: U.S. online adults.

Source: Forrester's North American Technographics Empowerment Online Survey, Q4 2009 (US).

apply, in which 80 percent of the influence comes from 20 percent of the consumers.[11]

It's actually much more extreme than that.

Among social connectors, 80 percent of the impressions about products and services come from only 6.2 percent of the people online (see figure 3-1). That's 11 million very connected people. These are the Mass Connectors.

Here's why you should care about Mass Connectors. First, they are 11 million people who generate, collectively, 205 billion impressions annually on other people regarding products and services. That's 18,600 impressions per Mass Connector per year. They have a lot of friends—the average Mass Connector has a total of 537 followers, friends, or connections in all of his or her social networks. (The rest of the social network members average 133.)

Social network impressions are fleeting, continuous, and viral. People retweet what others tweet, comment on others' Facebook updates, get influenced by what their best professional colleagues say on LinkedIn, and pass those messages on. More importantly, they're trusted, because they come from people's friends. (If you have 537 friends, they won't all be close friends, but even the acquaintances are more likely to pay attention to what you say than they would to a stranger.) So any strategy for tapping into this group needs to keep them close, not just once, but over time.

TABLE 3-1

Demographics of Mass Connectors and Mass Mavens

	Online adults	Mass Connectors	Mass Mavens
Male/female	48%/52%	50%/50%	56%/44%
Age (avg.)	44	32	38
Household income (avg.)	$79,100	$98,100	$89,800
Family/friends often or always seek their opinion	27%	50%	49%
Mobile Internet user (at least weekly)	25%	55%	46%

Base: U.S. online adults.

Source: Forrester's North American Technographics Empowerment Online Survey, Q4 2009 (US).

Let's try to understand these people better.

Half are men and half are women (see table 3-1). They're generally young, with an average age of thirty-two, and affluent, with an average household income of almost $100,000.

They think of themselves as influential—half of them say friends and family often seek their opinions. And 55 percent of them use the mobile Internet weekly, more than twice the population average.

We can also tell you where they are expressing their influence. Facebook is huge. For every ten impressions created in social networks in the United States, six come from Facebook, two come from MySpace, one comes from Twitter, and one comes from some other site (see figure 3-2).

But when it comes to influence, the Mass Connectors tell only half the story. To get the other half, we need to look at the people who make a more lasting impression: the Mass Mavens.

Mass Mavens create more lasting influence

In contrast to Mass Connectors, who make their impressions on others within social networks, Mass Mavens contribute to blogs, discussion forums, and online reviews. They generally don't know the people who see what they write, but their contributions can impress thousands

FIGURE 3-2

Most of the influence impressions within social networks come from Facebook

Share of influence impressions

Base: U.S. online adults.

Source: Forrester's North American Technographics Empowerment Online Survey, Q4 2009 (US).

of people over time. They're the other source of influence in the groundswell. So let's take a closer look at Mass Mavens.

About 13.4 percent of the U.S. online population, or 24 million people, are Mass Mavens (see figure 3-3). (About 7 million people are in the overlap, being both Mass Mavens and Mass Connectors.) By definition, Mass Mavens generate 80 percent of the online posts (blog posts, blog comments, discussion forums, and reviews) regarding products and services, or about 1.31 billion total posts every year. That's a

FIGURE 3-3

Mass Mavens account for 80 percent of the online posts about products and services

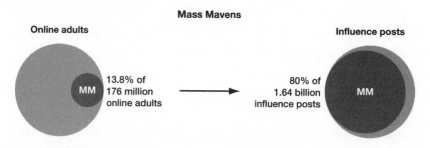

Base: U.S. online adults.

Source: Forrester's North American Technographics Empowerment Online Survey, Q4 2009 (US).

FIGURE 3-4

The majority of influence posts are on reviews and discussion forums

Share of influence posts

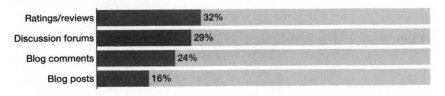

Ratings/reviews	32%
Discussion forums	29%
Blog comments	24%
Blog posts	16%

Base: U.S. online adults.
Source: Forrester's North American Technographics Empowerment Online Survey, Q4 2009 (US).

lot of content about stuff you may be selling. And because Google is biased toward content with a lot of inbound links, like blogs and discussion forums, many of these posts may end up near the top of the search rankings for your products or product categories.

In contrast to the Mass Connectors, the Mass Mavens are a little older, with an average age of thirty-eight, and not quite as rich, with an average income of $90,000. But like the Mass Connectors, they're often consulted by their friends and families and very likely to use the mobile Web.

What sets these people apart is their productivity. They have opinions and they love to spread them. The average Mass Maven posts content about products and services fifty-four times per year. (Others, if they post at all, average only six posts per year.)

As it turns out, blogging gets all the publicity, but discussion forums and ratings and reviews account for over 60 percent of the posts about products and services (see figure 3-4). And Mass Mavens contribute more blog comments than blog posts. So if you're monitoring online discussions about your products or using a service like Sysomos to do the monitoring for you, broaden your focus beyond blog posts, or you'll miss five-sixths of the comments people make.

peer influence varies by product category

Both the Mass Connectors and the Mass Mavens must be part of any influence strategy.

To tap the Mass Connectors, you need content they'll want to spread and link to, like viral videos or coupons. Comments from your own Twitter feeds and content from your Facebook pages are catnip for these types. You'll also want to monitor what they're saying, to make sure you can respond if there's a problem (like Best Buy's Coral Biegler did in chapter 1).

The Mass Mavens need to be handled a little differently. Because they write things like blog posts and reviews, they're a little more thoughtful. Making available as much information as possible makes those posts easier to write. This is why your own corporate blog, clearly usable product pages, and information in media matter when it comes time to influence Mass Mavens.

Of course, Mass Connectors and Mass Mavens don't talk equally about all brands in all categories (see figure 3-5). For example, United Airlines would need to know that 11 percent of online consumers comment on airline tickets. Doing the same sort of peer influence analysis on airline influence that we did for the overall population, we can tell that when it comes to airline comments specifically, 0.9 percent of online adults are Mass Connectors and 2.2 percent are Mass Mavens. Clearly, a small number of people (like Dave Carroll) have an outsized amount of influence.

United has learned its lesson; it's monitoring Twitter and has sixty thousand followers at @unitedairlines. (It turns out people who talk online about airlines are twice as likely to use Twitter as the general population.) It's also monitoring airline forums like flyertalk.com and blogs that talk about airlines, to see what airline Mass Mavens may be saying.

But influence analysis isn't just about defense—protecting your brand. It's also about spreading positive word of mouth with mass influencers. That's what Ford was aiming for when it launched the new Fiesta.

CASE STUDY

mass influencers for Ford

Here's Scott Monty's problem. Ford is an iconic American company. It's been around a long time. People think they know what Ford is, and

FIGURE 3-5

What people share opinions about on the Web

Which of the following are you likely to express your opinion about using the Web?

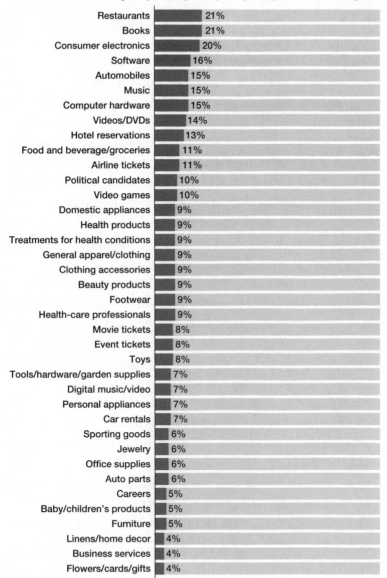

Restaurants	21%
Books	21%
Consumer electronics	20%
Software	16%
Automobiles	15%
Music	15%
Computer hardware	15%
Videos/DVDs	14%
Hotel reservations	13%
Food and beverage/groceries	11%
Airline tickets	11%
Political candidates	10%
Video games	10%
Domestic appliances	9%
Health products	9%
Treatments for health conditions	9%
General apparel/clothing	9%
Clothing accessories	9%
Beauty products	9%
Footwear	9%
Health-care professionals	9%
Movie tickets	8%
Event tickets	8%
Toys	8%
Tools/hardware/garden supplies	7%
Digital music/video	7%
Personal appliances	7%
Car rentals	7%
Sporting goods	6%
Jewelry	6%
Office supplies	6%
Auto parts	6%
Careers	5%
Baby/children's products	5%
Furniture	5%
Linens/home decor	4%
Business services	4%
Flowers/cards/gifts	4%

Base: U.S. online adults.

Source: Forrester's North American Technographics Empowerment Online Survey, Q4 2009 (US).

that image is old and stodgy. It doesn't help that the other two big American car companies, GM and Chrysler, drove themselves into a ditch and needed government bailouts, tarnishing the American automotive industry's image in the process.

Ford has a potential hit on its hands with the new Fiesta. This shiny and innovative new model was the second most popular vehicle in Europe in 2009. The company needed a way to raise excitement in advance of the Fiesta's U.S. launch in the summer of 2010.

So Scott and the team at Ford decided to manufacture some customers. Starting in 2009, they recruited a hundred people (including a few two-person teams) and gave them new Fiestas to drive around in. Daniel Grozdich is a working-class comedian in Malibu, California.[12] Kristina Horner is a student from Seattle who travels around the country with her band. Taylor Barr and David Parsons are road-trippers from North Carolina who love social networks. Ford reviewed four thousand applications and picked the one hundred who seemed most likely to drive the car around and talk about it.

Want to see what they're up to? Click on the live feed at www.fiesta movement.com. Between April and November of 2009, the fiesta movement's YouTube videos racked up 7 million views. Seven hundred thousand saw the pictures they posted on Flickr. Four million saw their tweets. Ford had packaged up the energy of these new Fiesta drivers and harnessed it for marketing.

It worked. One hundred thousand people who went to fiestamove ment.com signed up for a list to get more information. In December, the site began taking reservations. In one month, four thousand people signed up to buy a Fiesta.

Ford and Scott are not stopping now. In the next stage, volunteer Fiesta lovers will sign up in different parts of the country and channel the social activity by region. Because Scott knows that getting customers talking is the key to reinvigorating the image of Ford in America.

analyzing peer influence for Ford

Let's look at customer influence from Ford's point of view. Was the company's strategy to generate word of mouth with customers the right one? Here's where we can do an analysis of peer influence, not for general influencers, but for people who talk about cars.

First, let's look at people who talk online about cars, which includes about 15 percent of the online population in the United States. Car influencers are more tightly concentrated than general influencers, but not quite as much as airline influencers. Mass Connectors for cars are 1.3 percent of the online population, and Mass Mavens for cars are 3.4 percent (see figure 3-6).

We can also look at the other side of influence—not just what people are saying, but what they are checking. People getting ready to buy a car are most likely to say they check online ratings, news sites, and friends' opinions. Fewer *say* they check blogs or friends' opinions on social network sites. But remember, this is a process that starts with awareness (that might come from a blog post found in a search, a friend's tweet, or a news article written about fiestamovement.com).

FIGURE 3-6

Mass Mavens and Mass Connectors among car influencers

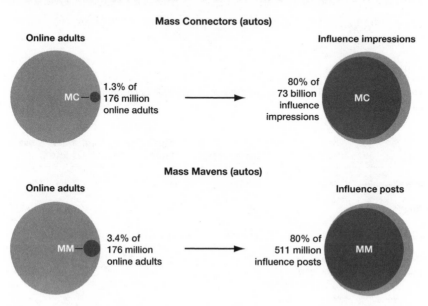

Base: U.S. online adults.

Source: Forrester's North American Technographics Empowerment Online Survey, Q4 2009 (US).

After the buyer becomes aware of the new Fiesta, she'll research sources like ratings sites and news sites. Ford doesn't want people *not* to check online information sites. It wants them to become aware of the Fiesta from as many sources as possible, and *then* check those sites.

Ford's challenge is this: the people who talk about cars are well off and influential, but rarely own Fords (see table 3-2). With this analysis, and based on what Scott Monty told me—that the Fiesta is intended for a new, mostly younger type of customer—you can see why Fiesta Movement had to be designed the way it was. Ford had to create customers by letting them drive the cars for a while, to prime the pump and get the discussion going.

influence by generation

Is the groundswell a youth movement?

The social technology world is skewed toward the young, but not as much as it used to be. In 2009, 73 percent of online consumers aged 18 to 24 were using social content at least once a month.[13] The corresponding number among consumers aged 45 to 54: 67 percent. Every year, the average age of social technology participants gets older.

TABLE 3-2

Demographics of Mass Connectors and Mass Mavens for auto purchases

	Online adults	Mass Connectors (autos)	Mass Mavens (autos)
Male/female	48%/52%	65%/35%	63%/37%
Age (avg.)	44	31	39
Household income (avg.)	$79,100	$104,100	$98,700
Own a Ford (most recently purchased/leased vehicle)	12%	3%	11%

Base: U.S. online adults.

Source: Forrester's North American Technographics Empowerment Online Survey, Q4 2009 (US).

How does this translate to peer influence? We analyzed three groups of people online—18-to-24-year-old young adults, 25-to-44-year-old mainstream consumers, and 45-and-older mature consumers. Is one of these groups your market? Then you need to know these facts:

- Youths share disproportionately, but don't dominate peer influence (see figure 3-7). While young adults are only 12 percent of the online population, they account for 30 percent of the influence impressions in social networks and 16 percent of the influence posts on blogs, forums, and reviews. The mainstream group of 25-to-44-year-old consumers generates more than half of the opinions about products and services in social environments of all kinds. And on blog, forum, and review sites, one in four opinions comes from consumers 45 and older.

- We looked at these separate pools of influence to identify the mass influencers among them. Thirteen percent of young adults are Mass Connectors and 18 percent are Mass Mavens, so mass influencers among youth are broader and less concentrated than those in the general online population (see figure 3-8). But because there are fewer active participants among consumers

FIGURE 3-7

Young adults have disproportionate influence, especially in social networks

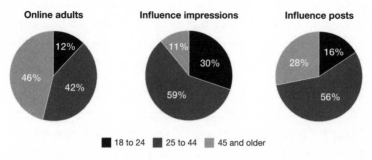

Base: U.S. online adults.

Source: Forrester's North American Technographics Empowerment Online Survey, Q4 2009 (US).

FIGURE 3-8

Mass Connectors and Mass Mavens among online consumers age 18 to 24

Mass Connectors (age 18 to 24)

Online adults

Influence impressions

MC

12.5% of
22 million
online adults

80% of
77 billion
influence
impressions

MC

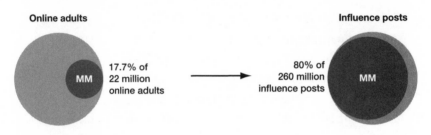

Mass Mavens (age 18 to 24)

Online adults

Influence posts

MM

17.7% of
22 million
online adults

80% of
260 million
influence posts

MM

Base: U.S. online adults age 18 to 24.
Source: Forrester's North American Technographics Empowerment Online Survey, Q4 2009 (US).

forty-five and over, the Mass Mavens and Mass Connectors in this group are much more tightly defined: only 3.7 percent of online adults forty-five and over are Mass Connectors, and only 12.9 percent are Mass Mavens (see figure 3-9).

• Looking at share of influence in social networks, Facebook is the biggest source of social network influence for all ages, but MySpace is second for young adults, while Twitter is second for mature consumers. On social content sites, young adults spend more effort on blogs and blog comments, while mature consumers are disproportionately likely to express their opinions on ratings sites.

FIGURE 3-9

Mass Connectors and Mass Mavens among adults 45 and over

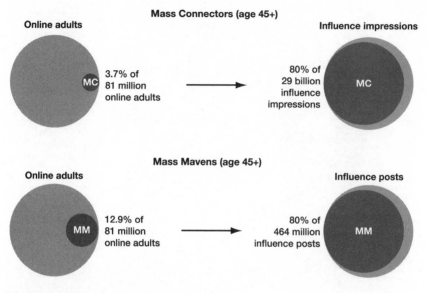

Base: U.S. online adults age 45 and older.

Source: Forrester's North American Technographics Empowerment Online Survey, Q4 2009 (US).

what peer influence means: customers matter more *after* the sale

We all remember the marketing funnel from Marketing 101. In the funnel, people become aware of your company, consider its products, and then a few of them buy. (In more recent versions of the funnel, "loyalty" is at the narrow end.)

But now the mass influencers among your customers are broadcasting information about your products. The more empowered they get, the more influence they have. Increasingly, it's their voice, not yours, that fellow buyers will hear.

This suggests a different view of the funnel, one in which sales is no longer the endpoint. Once you have sold a customer, good service will create happiness. Surrounding them with information will generate more touchpoints, and more reasons to feel good about your company. And enough outreach like this will create a customer who broadcasts your praises (see figure 3-10).[14]

FIGURE 3-10

In the new marketing funnel, influence begins *after* the sale

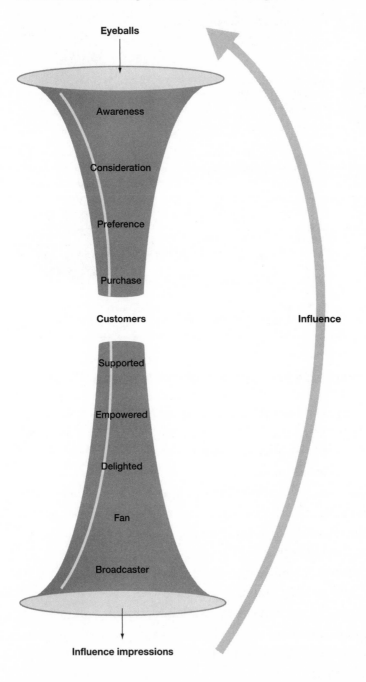

Let's put this in context with a personal story. I (Josh) like to travel with my family. Hotels are too cramped for us. I like to rent a bigger place. So a few years ago, I found a Web site called rentvillas.com that has hundreds of houses throughout Europe. I arranged to rent a house in Italy.

Renting a house in another country can be nerve-wracking. To help you through the process, Rentvillas assigns you a personal travel advisor. Ours emailed me and then responded to questions about everything from local supermarkets to clothes dryers. She also sent us a map and a little 150-page self-published paperback by the company's founder, Suzanne Pidduck, on living in Italy.

Our stay was delightful. After I returned, Suzanne emailed to suggest we rate the property on Rentvillas' site. And after we'd done that, she suggested we rate the property on some other online travel sites, like ricksteves.com. The email was personal—it actually mentioned the minor problems we'd described with the Italian property. I later learned she sends hundreds of those emails every week.

Rentvillas manages two thousand rentals a year. I had already paid. And yet here the company was, treating me as important even though my next trip was certainly years off.

Rentvillas got my loyalty. But they got more, because I'm a Mass Maven. When they sent me the most deliciously tempting newsletter I've ever read, I blogged it.[15] And when I wanted to hold up examples of companies that treat their customers like human beings, I interviewed Suzanne and blogged about it again. And here I am writing about it.

Rentvillas didn't target me after carefully measuring my level of influence. They simply reached out to me, a customer, since they knew that my word of mouth, in person and online, would influence others. Just as they do with all the other customers.

Suzanne has recognized that the funnel doesn't stop at the narrow end; it continues with personal service, surrounding the customer with information resources, and encouraging word of mouth. Customers are a marketing channel. Especially influential ones. Shiv Singh, vice president and global social media lead for Razorfish, calls this social influence marketing, or "having your customers create customers for you."

If you think this philosophy can't apply in big companies, you haven't accounted for the employee HEROes who come up with solutions like Suzanne's emails and Scott Monty's Ford Fiesta Movement. You just need to find ways to encourage your staff to think this way.

In the next three chapters we describe those ways: delivering groundswell customer service, empowering customers with information, and amplifying word of mouth (the D, E, and A in IDEA). And we show how to do it efficiently, regardless of the size of your company.

4. delivering groundswell customer service

In June of 2004, I (Josh) was in a midtown Manhattan conference room presenting to six of the men who originally created the cable television industry. One was Ralph Roberts, the founder of Comcast, who can only be described as dapper in his ever-present bowtie. Ralph and his son, Brian, had created the most powerful cable company on the planet.

My job that day was to present ideas about the future of television, but one of my PowerPoint slides showed customer satisfaction levels among different operators based on Forrester's Technographics consumer surveys. Among major operators, Comcast was at the bottom.[1] Ralph cringed as his fellow cable barons looked on.

Three years later, Comcast had swallowed up enough cable systems to grow to 24 million customers, with financially healthy businesses like digital phone, broadband Internet, HDTV, and video on demand. But Comcast was about to be flanked between low-cost satellite providers like Dish Network and shiny new TV/broadband/phone offerings from Verizon and AT&T. Poor service could lead to defections.

In 2007, Comcast's service problems began to become highly visible and embarrassing in the groundswell. A video of a technician who'd come to fix a customer's cable modem, then fell asleep on his couch, racked up over a million views on YouTube.[2] *Advertising Age* columnist and NPR commentator Bob Garfield started a blog for Comcast complainers, comcastmustdie.com, and gathered 191 comments on his very first post.[3] And as reported in the *Washington Post,* Mona Shaw, a seventy-five-year-old Virginia grandmother, became so frustrated with ongoing service interruptions that she went down to the local cable office with a claw hammer and smashed every bit of equipment in sight.[4]

When grandmothers go on rampages, you've got a problem. The company tossed out some of its contract service technicians and telephone support staff and replaced them with its own staff. New technology systems empowered the service staff to make problem detection and solution easier. By 2009, Comcast was able to solve four out of five problems on the first phone call.

Unfortunately, many of the customers still remembered the Comcast service that had made Ralph Roberts cringe. So the company became open to a new kind of service—groundswell customer service—that could not only satisfy customers, but also get them talking.

Frank Eliason, a highly empowered and resourceful operative in the company's service operation, had begun to reach out to complaining customers on blogs and through the Twitter alias @comcastcares. The result, frequently, was positive comments from those customers in the same channels. In February 2008, when the company offered to make outreach to customers through social sites his full-time job, he was excited to take on the challenge. Go ahead; if you have Comcast, tweet your problems to @comcastcares, and Frank's likely to answer.

Frank and his digital care team of ten service staffers, now reporting to the head of customer service, have been doing this longer than just about anyone else in the service space. Service is a serious, high-volume activity at Comcast, and they do it efficiently. They have a billing person and a broadband expert. They go through Twitter, blogs, and discussion forums. They even look on Facebook groups for people who *hate* Comcast. They respond to six thousand emails a month that are sent to we_can_help@comcast.com. If you're complaining about Comcast and they can detect it through search, monitoring, or any other way, they'll reach out to you.

Why? Because making customers happy creates word of mouth. "A lot of people will tweet before they get home to make the call," Frank explains. "We reach out at that point. That's less time for them to fester and be angry." And you never know which customer may turn out to be Mona Shaw and her hammer.

If they can do groundswell customer service, so can you.

The constant monitoring has generated unexpected dividends. For example, in April 2009, during an NHL playoff game, Frank noticed a spike in complaints about Comcast and the NHL on Twitter—and it became clear that the game broadcast had disappeared from TV screens throughout Pennsylvania. Frank did a quick check and saw there were also complaints on Twitter about DIRECTV. He deduced that the problem was with the channel originating the broadcast, Fox Sports Net in Atlanta, and not with Comcast.

In minutes, he sent an alert to Comcast's telephone service team, giving them the information they would need when calls started to pour in. He also arranged for the message played for callers on hold to explain that the problem was Fox Sports Net, and that Comcast couldn't fix it. In the half hour it took for the broadcast to be restored, the digital service team had headed off hundreds of phone calls and helped Comcast avoid blame for a problem it hadn't caused.

The digital care team is a highly visible part of Comcast's service operation—dozens of articles have been written about it, in places like *BusinessWeek* and the *Wall Street Journal*. This not only provides a counterweight to stories of grandmothers with hammers, it also helps to inspire the rest of Comcast's thousands of service employees as they see that Comcast is getting credit for improved service. According to the American Customer Satisfaction Index, an independent group that measures service attitudes, Comcast's scores increased five percentage points between 2008 and 2009.

Comcast wants the story out that its service is improving. The digital care team is a part of that. Because when customers are empowered, customer service is marketing.

why customer service is marketing

Comcast empowered Frank Eliason's team to solve customer problems. He's a HERO all right. But how can we say that customer service is now marketing?

Marketing reaches masses and sells. Marketing is for people who aren't customers yet. Once they become customers, customer service kicks in. Customer service is individualized and costly. That doesn't sound like marketing.

Except that empowered customers talk, they blog, they Twitter, and they post reviews and videos. Remember Rentvillas.com's customers from the previous chapter? Suzanne Pidduck kept them happy to keep them talking. That's what Frank Eliason wants, too—happy customers talking. He wants to energize those customers in a positive way, to harness the power of their word of mouth.

What exactly is customer service? The job of the customer service team is to route the customer efficiently to a place where she can get the information she needs or get her problem solved. But a focus on reducing costs has created problems. Twenty years ago when corporations first adopted customer service technologies, without meaning to, they set up customer service to fail. Cost-cutting strategies defined customers' questions and concerns as a nuisance to be dealt with in the most minimal way possible. They focused only on efficiency and forgot about the value of the customer experience.[5] This focus on low-cost, uniform service gave us touch-tone menus, Web sites, and outsourcing. If you're the square peg—the person with a problem that doesn't fit the system—then you're adding cost. Including the grandma with the hammer.

What is marketing? There are a thousand definitions, but one is this: marketing is getting ideas about a company and its products out to as many people as possible, in the hopes of converting them to customers. Here again, marketing is a cost, so it pays to be efficient. Efficiency means treating everyone pretty much the same. Broadcast the TV ad, buy the search term on Google, but whatever you do, do it efficiently. Create customers in bunches, then move on.

But now, some of your customers are Mass Connectors and Mass Mavens. They talk. Their voices, taken together, are more persuasive than any ad campaign. This is why "delivering groundswell customer service" is the second step—the *D*—in IDEA. Because solving customer problems, making customers happy, and harnessing their power to talk about it *is* marketing. Customer service is marketing.

a new service discipline: groundswell customer service

Viewing customer service as marketing means a change in the way you approach both disciplines. You don't have to throw away your customer service tools and systems, and you don't have to jettison your current marketing. The key to turning customer service into a marketing channel is to be *efficient*, like Comcast's digital care team.

In this context, it's important to note that the first problem to solve is not the groundswell problem—it's the service problem. Comcast had to make big and expensive changes to its poor service before its groundswell strategy could make a difference. But once the traditional service is better, customer service that features outreach through social channels can energize word of mouth from those happier customers.

We call this new kind of service *groundswell customer service*. It's a customer service discipline in which your staff connect with customers wherever they're making noise—on Twitter, blogs, or YouTube, for example—and help them, thereby turning them into broadcasters of positive messages. Here's what you need to do to create a groundswell customer service system:

- *Listen.* Use a tool like Visible Technologies' TruVoice or Radian6 to identify people talking about your brand, your company, or your industry. Many of the companies that make customer service routing and tracking software used in call centers are adding these features; RightNow Technologies is one such firm. Until you know what people are saying, you don't know where to start. And until you have a tool like this in place, you can't be efficient in addressing online service issues.

- *Staff and organize to address service issues.* Comcast has a small social engagement team within a larger service organization. If you've got a large service group now, you'll likely need additional people to cover all the new channels in the groundswell, as Frank's team does. But as you'll see in the rest of this chapter, because groundswell customer service is marketing, it generates a range of organizational models in different departments. The key, regardless of which way you organize, is to create an efficient system that not only addresses service issues, but helps turn them into word-of-mouth marketing opportunities.

- *Concentrate on the experience.* When customer service is seen as a cost, the main objective is to deal with people quickly. But once you see it as a way to create marketing resonance, the focus shifts. All customer service should have the goal of improving the experience for customers, with the objective of getting them to spread positive word of mouth. In contrast to traditional customer service, groundswell customer service is a process challenge, since any customer might turn into Dave "United Breaks Guitars" Carroll. When evaluating different process designs, ask, "What's most likely to improve the customer experience?" Choose designs—and metrics—based on this concept.

- *Plan to evolve.* The groundswell is changing. As we write this, Twitter is a key element in groundswell customer service, because it's so immediate and easy to search. But as social technology evolves—and as organizations learn to participate—your efforts will grow and evolve as well. So will their connections to your traditional service and marketing activities. So don't get too comfortable. The employee HEROes who implement these systems need to review them every six months or so with an eye toward adjusting them to new technologies and tools that customers are adopting.

diverse models of groundswell customer service

We'd like to give you a peek into two more groundswell customer service models in different industries, with different types of customers, using different technologies. These examples show different organizational models for groundswell customer service: whereas Comcast has a separate team for it, the small business software division of Intuit has made it part of marketing, and the online shoe retailer Zappos weaves service into its core values for all departments.

What these examples share is an awareness on the part of marketers and service managers that they can't just sit in their call centers and wait for customers to come to them—they must reach out and help customers with problems throughout the groundswell. As you read these cases, have a look at the different ways the participants measure value, and how they redefine what service means.

CASE STUDY

Intuit merges marketing, groundswell outreach, and product development

Kira Wampler hates silos.

Kira is online engagement leader for the small-business division of Intuit, the division that makes QuickBooks, a product that millions of small businesses use for accounting. Unlike Frank Eliason, she's in marketing. But her job crosses lots of boundaries. She owns the popular support communities that QuickBooks runs so that small-business people can get accounting help from each other. She creates social media marketing campaigns. Add the Twitter feed and the Facebook page, and she and her twelve staffers have plenty to do.

But that isn't enough for Kira, because she recognizes that brand perceptions, product features, and marketing are intertwined. Take Web traffic. "The marketer in me would expect to spend huge sums of money to get traffic to the product marketing site," she says. "But when I saw all the traffic that goes from our communities to the marketing site, I literally fell off my chair." A site designed for support was generating sales. Customer service really *is* marketing.

So Kira and her colleagues expanded the connections among product development, groundswell customer service, and marketing. In July 2009, she and her managers broke down the walls and made one big group. While traditional customer support remains separate from these marketing functions, Kira and her team have a strong working relationship with support, too.

What does this mean? Let's look at an example. Kira's group saw that a lot of the conversation about QuickBooks was happening on Amazon.com, in the ratings and reviews for the product. The reviews were mixed; over 30 percent were neutral or negative. And the negatives were pretty consistent. Take this one, from a customer going by "R. Pink Floyd":[6]

> Quick[B]ooks is a nice program in many ways. It's easy to use, clean, produces quality documents . . . But my biggest problem with it is that the entire program just seems highly focused on sucking money out of the customer. Things that should be basic features require pricey subscriptions . . . This year, before I got the program I was impressed when reading about the feature that allows you to attach documents to a customer or vendor . . . But then I get the program and I find that they CHARGE you to store docs.

The basic complaint was one they were also hearing from other places: that QuickBooks had too many "hooks" asking customers to spend money to upgrade features. Because of the flexibility of her new team, Kira could now solve this problem in multiple ways.

First, she asked her people to monitor Amazon and respond to every single comment there. Here's how Bryan on her team responded on behalf of Intuit:

> This is Community_Bryan from Intuit . . . Just wanted to let you know that the Document Management feature is free up to 100MB. There is only a charge if you store more than 100MB total, and that is totally an optional service. Please email me at community_bryan@intuit.com if I can help with anything else.
>   Respectfully, Bryan

She could also bring influence from these customers to bear on the product development people. The evidence from Amazon and elsewhere now was very persuasive that features intended to help users were being perceived as too hard-sell. So product development shifted its priorities, and the next version of QuickBooks will go much easier on the cross-selling.

Another example: the traditional way to think about support forums is that they help reduce support costs by letting people answer each others' questions. Kira rejects this idea, since as a marketer she wants to boost word of mouth by making more happy customers. So for her, the key metric is not calls avoided, it's issues resolved. "The job of these [communities] is not call deflection," she explains. "That's the worst measure of the site. My job is: how do I get you unstuck as quickly as possible?"

As a result, if you post a question on the support forum and there's no answer from other forum members within forty-eight hours, you'll see a reply from Intuit featuring the toll-free number, and a suggestion to call for help. Intuit *wants* you to call. Sure, it increases call volume, but it means more people happy with the product.

Intuit is well down the road of embracing social technologies—it is one of only two companies (the other is Dell) that Forrester Research has recognized for the companywide transformation that comes from embracing social technologies in everything from marketing to product innovation.[7] As we'll describe in chapter 9, this comes in part from the leadership of Intuit founder Scott Cook, who recognizes that getting people to re-up on his software products every year requires a relentless focus on customer satisfaction. The small-business division's ability to break down silos was possible because social applications—and the voice of the customer—had wormed their way into so many parts of the company. So now, at Intuit, customer support is marketing. And that makes Kira happy, because she hates silos.

if you sell to small business, marketing and customer service need to connect

How do small-business owners decide on software? This is a pretty important question for the Intuit small-business team.

The peer influence analysis of small-business customers reveals what Intuit is doing right. Twenty million people online work for businesses with fewer than ten employees. One in sixteen is a Mass Connector, and one in six is a Mass Maven (see figure 4-1). Except for their above-average use of mobile technology, the mass influencers group is quite typical of small-business employees in their incomes, age, gender split, and the places they share their opinions. You might guess that small-business employees love to share on LinkedIn, but it turns out they share in the same channels as everybody else—Facebook, Twitter, ratings and

FIGURE 4-1

Mass influencers among small-business employees

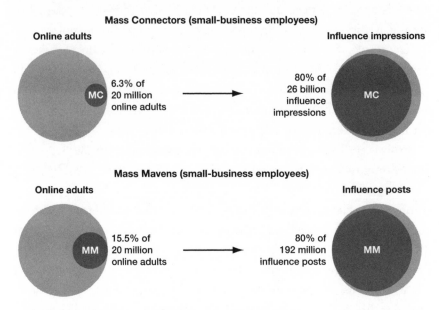

Mass Connectors (small-business employees)

Online adults

Influence impressions

MC

6.3% of
20 million
online adults

80% of
26 billion
influence
impressions

MC

Mass Mavens (small-business employees)

Online adults

Influence posts

MM

15.5% of
20 million
online adults

80% of
192 million
influence posts

MM

Base: U.S. information workers in businesses with fewer than 10 employees.
Source: Forrester's North American Technographics Empowerment Online Survey, Q4 2009 (US).

reviews, and discussion forums (see figure 4-2). (While they also share in MySpace, it's probably not software they're discussing there.)

Intuit's QuickBooks folks already had some of the most popular discussion forums for small business. This analysis reveals why they began to focus on Amazon ratings as well. And it also demonstrates why they have to concentrate on service—because it's so hard to distinguish the mass influencers in this market from others, it makes sense to treat every customer as a potential influencer, and every online post as a source of that influence.

When customers are sharing—and any customer could be a source of referral—it pays to combine customer service and marketing. Should marketing and customer service go together at your company?

Unless your business is pretty small, or has embraced the groundswell the way Intuit has, you probably can't break down the boundaries between customer service and marketing. But you can build bridges.

FIGURE 4-2

Small-business buyers use similar channels to other online consumers

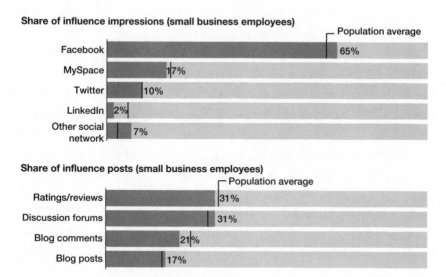

Share of influence impressions (small business employees)

		Population average
Facebook		65%
MySpace	17%	
Twitter	10%	
LinkedIn	2%	
Other social network	7%	

Share of influence posts (small business employees)

		Population average
Ratings/reviews		31%
Discussion forums		31%
Blog comments	21%	
Blog posts	17%	

Base: Information workers in businesses with fewer than ten employees.
Source: Forrester's North American Technographics Empowerment Online Survey, Q4 2009 (US).

The key is to put the customer at the center. Groundswell customer service surfaces what's on customers' minds. You can solve their immediate problem, which creates word of mouth. And you can solve their ultimate problem, by changing your company to serve them better.

online communities and customer service

Intuit's communities, which Kira manages, are quite an asset to the company's customer service. Communities with forums are great—if your products are complex and your customers share issues, you should start one (or support one your customers have already started elsewhere on the Web). We've seen successful corporate-run communities for everything from environmental professionals to owners of robot vacuum cleaners. Lithium and Awareness Networks are two of a host of vendors that will be happy to set you up with one. But the key is to approach communities properly. While customers really do solve each other's problems in these environments, support managers should concentrate on how they can improve the company's reputation for service, generate insights about products, and locate the most enthusiastic backers of the company, not just deflect costs.

Online communities can solve other problems, too. We recently spoke to Barry Paperno, who runs the community forums for FICO[8] (formerly Fair Isaac), a company that provides credit scores to consumers. FICO can provide scores, but it can't provide advice on how to improve those scores—if it did, financial regulators would classify it as a "credit repair agency" and impose an onerous set of additional regulations. Naturally, though, people interested in credit scores want to understand and improve them as they recover from financial problems and attempt to qualify for loans, credit cards, or mortgages. The FICO community solves that problem for FICO—it creates an environment where customers can provide advice to one another about improving credit.

As with Intuit, FICO benefits from the community activity. Potential customers spend 66 percent more at FICO after registering for the forum, and 13 percent of all FICO's online sales involve viewing a community page. Community forums have another benefit, too—like all link-rich social activity, they increase sites' rankings in Google and other search engines. Partly as a result of the forum, 39 percent of all the traffic to FICO's online site now comes from unpaid placement in search engines, which is yet another way that customer service becomes marketing.

Of course, the apotheosis of customer service is when service is not just a corporate function, but a corporate value. Many companies pay lip service to this ideal; few attain it. Perhaps the most visibly successful is the online retailer Zappos.

CASE STUDY

Zappos's love affair with customers

At Zappos, customer service isn't marketing, it's everything.

Here are the company's core values, developed by the employees themselves and used in evaluating hires:[9]

1. Deliver WOW Through Service

2. Embrace and Drive Change

3. Create Fun and a Little Weirdness

4. Be Adventurous, Creative, and Open-Minded

5. Pursue Growth and Learning

6. Build Open and Honest Relationships with Communication

7. Build a Positive Team and Family Spirit

8. Do More with Less

9. Be Passionate and Determined

10. Be Humble

Service is value number one. Number two and number four, "Embrace and Drive Change" and "Be Adventurous, Creative, and Open-Minded," might as well read "be an employee HERO." And this isn't just lip service. When you talk to people who work at Zappos, you recognize that they fundamentally believe in these values. This service reputation drove Zappos to $1 billion in sales, and led to its acquisition by Amazon at a valuation of over $1 billion. Amazon will be retaining the Zappos brand, because Zappos's service reputation is a big part of what Amazon coveted.

What does a brand built around a "wow" level of service look like?

For one thing, Zappos doesn't advertise much. Instead, it invests in service. Since the main hurdles in buying shoes and clothes online are that they might not fit or look the way you hoped, Zappos provides free shipping and free returns. Frequently, customers find themselves upgraded to one- or two-day shipping for nothing.

The call center and the Web site are the face of Zappos, the front-lines of "wow." The phone number is listed at the top of the Web site and answered twenty-four hours a day, seven days a week. Eighty percent of calls are answered within twenty seconds.

That's service, but it's not absurd service. For absurd service, try this: Zappos customer Wendy Fitch had already bought a pair of heels from Zappos, asked for and received a credit when she found out they were available more cheaply from another store, and blogged about it. A few weeks later, she went on a three-day breast cancer walk and set her email to automatically respond "Thanks for your e-mail. I am currently hitting the pavement in Denver, walking 60 miles in three days to put an end to breast cancer. I'll respond to your e-mail when I'm back." A Zappos service staffer noticed this autoresponse in the Zappos inbox and sent a handwritten note:

THANK YOU

Hello Wendy!

While working through emails from our amazing customers, I came across your auto reply . . . I just wanted to let you know what an admirable thing you are doing! We at Zappos are proud to have you as a customer, and as part of our family.

Thank you for being a wonderful person.

Ashlee—customer relations rep at Zappos

Naturally, Wendy blogged about Zappos again.[10] Here's an excerpt:

Zappos—you SERIOUSLY rock. I am in marketing/customer service shock. And if any of you have heard my recent complaints . . . you know I was starting to lose faith in customer service. I love that I can now gloat about a company that has gone above and beyond. I've made one purchase from Zappos.com. One. And this is what I get. Unfreaking believable. Now I don't have to feel guilty buying shoes, 'cause I'm gonna go hog wild at Zappos.com.

That's what happens when you deliver absurd service. And this is no one-off. People at Zappos do stuff like this all the time.

It's one thing to create a service culture like the one at Zappos. It's another to expose that service culture and make it a marketing asset. Zappos exposes its culture in multiple ways. For example, its CEO, Tony

Hsieh, is in high demand as a speaker, and has parlayed his customer activities and visibility into more than a million Twitter followers at @zappos.

All Zappos employees are trained in Twitter when they join up and encouraged to tweet about themselves and their jobs. In a more daring move, Twitter's site features a page with all the tweets that mention Zappos (twitter.zappos.com). Tweets like this are typical: " @jeffvanlan: ordered shoes last night at 6:30, got them this morning at 9:30. That's some Wow factor Zappos. Happy Holidays." Not every Tweet on this page is a thumbs up, but the mix is so overwhelmingly positive that you can't help but think this company does things right.

Service this good is expensive but it pays off, because Zappos runs service efficiently. The enthusiasm of the service teams, many of whom are happy to have these jobs in economically depressed Las Vegas, translates into high productivity. Turnover among the call center staff is an absurdly low 20 percent per year, far below what's typical in the industry. And the service Zappos delivers creates loyalty, which makes selling far easier. The average size of a customer's first order at Zappos is $125. The second order averages $145.

Maybe your company doesn't deliver anywhere near Zappos's level of service, so the tactics that Zappos uses are beyond you. But if you generally make customers happy, take a close look at the way Zappos turns customer happiness into loyalty, buzz, and word-of-mouth marketing. Once you've made them happy, get them talking.

the efficient approach to groundswell customer service

As you can see from Comcast, Intuit, and Zappos, your groundswell customer service strategy depends greatly on your company's reputation. If, like Zappos, you have a sterling service reputation, your goal should be to maintain it and encourage your customers to share their perspectives. If, like Intuit, you have some detractors, you can use groundswell customer service to respond to them and influence your company's products and policies in a more productive direction. And if you're climbing out of a hole, as Comcast was, then your social outreach team will be putting out fires, an activity that has its best long-term impact in the context of a complete service overhaul. But regardless, you'll need ways to do groundswell customer service *efficiently;* a one-off approach to these channels will bog you down. From what we've learned from these companies and many others, here are a few tips for how to make these techniques most effective:

- *Monitor and evaluate before building a strategy.* Often, these initiatives come into being because a company has its own "United Breaks Guitars" or Comcast Sleeping Technician moment. Resist the urge to build your service strategy when your blood is boiling. If you've got no groundswell presence yet, leave it to your PR department to clean up the mess. Then, after things have cooled off, start using listening tools and evaluating the share of peer influence of your customers, and use those insights to design a strategy.

- *Prepare with scale in mind.* Having monitored online activity for a little while, you can get a clearer idea of just how big a job you've got on your hands. How many tweets a day will you be handling? Are you going to monitor blogs, YouTube, and Facebook, too? Who will be responsible, and how much can they do in a day? And what happens nights, weekends, and vacations when they're not available? You'll need to develop efficient systems for responding to, handing over, and prioritizing outreach activity.

- *Get a crisis plan ready.* Things go wrong. Lightning strikes a transmitter in Atlanta and Comcast gets blamed for an NHL playoff outage. When events like this happen, positive or negative, your team will be overwhelmed with a surge of traffic. You need the equivalent of a big red emergency button, so any of your staff can initiate the crisis response. Your plan should include recalling off-duty staff, borrowing people from other departments, and triage to decide which responses are most urgently needed. Involve public relations staff in your planning, so they'll know how to work with you and the media in the midst of the maelstrom. While you can't prevent brand damage, you can mitigate it, provided you're prepared.

- *Make connections between service and marketing.* If you've made your groundswell customer service an extension of traditional service, then you'll want to collaborate with marketing staff around how to increase positive word of mouth and deal with fallout from detractors. Conversely, if your groundswell customer service is part of marketing, you'll need an efficient channel to do handoffs with your traditional call center and customer service systems.

- *Prepare the service wizards in other departments.* Your groundswell customer service team can't solve all the problems. They need to know who in your organization has the knowledge and authority to unravel billing snafus, solve technical problems, or reach out to people who've been treated insensitively by your staff. And those resources need to know that when a customer gets handed over, he's a priority, because he may soon be broadcasting the results of how he's treated.

- *Build streamlined systems.* Marketers are used to the need to get approval before publishing. Groundswell customer service happens in public, but your staff need the training and authority to be highly empowered and resourceful operatives—HEROes—to meet the challenge of the empowered customers they'll be serving. They can't wait for approvals. An appropriately designed system empowers each of your staff to connect with fifty or a hundred people a day and take appropriate action to solve their problems or route them to someone who can.

- *Create marketing metrics alongside your service metrics.* Unlike traditional service staff, don't measure your groundswell customer service efforts solely on the number of people served. Instead, look at long-term measures like shift in buzz sentiment from negative to positive, leads generated from Twitter and blogs, traffic to marketing pages, and positive customer stories.

keep customers happy by surrounding them with information

Customer service helps you find and serve people with problems. One way to keep those customers happy is to empower them—with information. And these days, mobile applications are the best way to do that, as we show in chapter 5.

5. empowering customers with mobile applications

Cindie Parmelee is an old hand in the stock market. She started as a secretary in a brokerage house decades ago, back when buy and sell orders came by phone or mailgram. She learned the business inside and out. But as the connections to the stock market accelerated, so did her idea of what she could do with it. For the last six years she's been a day trader working from her home in Atlanta, using a highly disciplined set of rules in a narrow set of high-volume NYSE stocks that earn enough to support her pretty well. After reviewing several brokers and systems, she settled on the trading setup from E*TRADE.

Her only problem was that her trading system and her PC had become a prison. If the market was open, she had to be at her system or she would miss opportunities. Things could shift while she was running an errand or picking up one of her kids at school. As she puts it, "I was tethered to my desk all day long."

One day in 2008 she found a way to cut the tether. E*TRADE announced an application for the BlackBerry and she bought one, three months before the app was due out. "I was so excited I couldn't stand it," she says. Since E*TRADE Mobile Pro for BlackBerry is based entirely on E*TRADE for the Web, Cindie now had the cues, alerts, and capabilities she needed to go mobile. Later that year, she boarded a plane bound for New York, sat down, and immediately used her BlackBerry to place a buy order with an instruction to sell at a given price. Ten minutes later, before the cabin doors had even closed, the sell order kicked in. She'd generated enough to pay for the flight. Other passengers wondered why she was pumping her fist as they streamed by to take their seats.

E*TRADE Mobile Pro came to market under the direction of Paul Vienick, senior VP of product development for E*TRADE. Research had proven that sophisticated mobile devices, including the Black-Berry, were rapidly penetrating its affluent, technically sophisticated customer base. Letters demanding the company's trading system on BlackBerry kept arriving at the company's offices. So in the summer of 2008, after just a few months of development, E*TRADE released the mobile application that delighted Cindie Parmelee.

Taking E*TRADE mobile has been good for business.

People are arriving, assets in hand, and saying they switched to get mobile trading. The mobile application continues to generate healthy and rapidly growing trading volumes. And it's not just traders. The company's "mass affluent" customers, who invest for the long term and trade much less frequently, are using the mobile application just to keep tabs on their investments.

E*TRADE Mobile Pro is now an essential part of the company's strategy.[1] The company's famous "talking baby" appeared in a 2009 Super Bowl ad to brag about how connected his BlackBerry and E*TRADE kept him (during the commercial, the phone rings and the baby has to tell his girlfriend he'll call her back). In May 2009, E*TRADE released an iPhone app, and found that iPhone owners loved E*TRADE Mobile Pro too, although it turns out they're not as transaction-oriented as the BlackBerry owners.

While it's challenging to keep up with the different mobile phone formats, Paul and E*TRADE plan to continue developing the applica-tion to support other devices, including the Google Android. "I did not expect it to take off as quickly as it did," Paul says. "We needed it. Cus-tomers were asking for it." After all, financial services is an information business. And these days, mobile customers expect that information to follow them everywhere.

who empowers your customers? it had better be you

The groundswell means that customers have more information power than ever before. Mobile browsing and mobile applications have made that power ubiquitous.

You have a choice to make. You can line yourself up with them, empowering them with mobile offers, mobile information, and mobile customer service. Or you can let them find that stuff on their own. In chapter 3, we saw that Mass Connectors and Mass Mavens are almost twice as likely to use the mobile Web as other consumers. Conversely, when we look at mobile Web users, they are far more likely to have influence. They're an attractive and influential group of consumers, from nearly every perspective (see table 5-1).

Mobile Web users expect you to be there. Empower them with information, and they'll talk about how great your company is. Don't, and they'll tell their friends you don't have a clue.

That's why empowering mobile customers is the third of the four steps you need to take to harness empowered customers, after identifying mass influencers and delivering groundswell customer service.

TABLE 5-1

Mobile Web users are a desirable group of consumers

| | | MOBILE WEB USERS (AT LEAST WEEKLY) | | | | |
	Online adults	All mobile Web	Mass Connectors	Mass Mavens	iPhone owners	BlackBerry owners
% of online adults	100%	22.5%	2.4%	4.2%	3.9%	7.4%
Male/female	48%/52%	55%/45%	52%/48%	60%/40%	56%/44%	59%/41%
Age (avg.)	44	37	30	35	37	39
Household income (avg.)	$79,100	$93,600	$114,100	$100,800	$111,000	$110,200
Friends/ family often or always seek their opinion	27%	39%	61%	62%	39%	40%

Base: U.S. online adults.

Source: Forrester's North American Technographics Empowerment Online Survey, Q4 2009 (US).

The need for mobile outreach is growing. In 2009, 34 million U.S. consumers used mobile phones to access the Internet; Forrester forecasts that number will reach 106 million by 2014.[2] In Western Europe, we expect mobile Internet penetration to reach 39 percent of mobile phone owners by 2014.[3] But it's not the mobile Internet that makes the difference to your company. It's the complete change in your customers' behavior.

E*TRADE customer Cindie Parmelee describes the feeling of leaving the house without her BlackBerry this way: "I felt like I had left one of my children somewhere." We love our mobile phones.

People with mobile data services use their smartphones more frequently, and become more attached to them. They use them to fill in the cracks in their day. Waiting for the elevator? Peek at the BlackBerry. Sitting in front of the TV? Whip out the iPhone. Waiting for a meeting to start (or even in the middle of the meeting, if it gets a little dull)? Open up the Droid.

What are they doing on those phones? Everything (see figure 5-1).

They're making movie choices. They're answering email. They're making social network contacts, Twittering, and texting. They're checking the customer ratings on your cowboy boots, determining whether the flight is on time and whether their friends are in the airport, reading a review of the restaurant they just drove by, or checking their progress against their workout and diet plans. If you have a relationship with a customer—if you market to them, sell to them, or service their account—they will expect you to be there on their mobile device.

The other thing to know about these mobile customers is that they are damned impatient. Since mobile devices fill cracks in the day, they need to answer questions *quickly*. Is that Dane Cook in the new TV series? What recipe includes pasta and capers but is low in fat? Am I experiencing heartburn or a heart attack? The people with these questions want answers *now*. If you're there for them, they will love you. If not, they're ready to work with somebody else.

As Forrester mobile analyst Julie A. Ask told me, "Right now, I can't name a *Fortune* 500 company that is *not* evaluating its mobile strategy."

FIGURE 5-1

Monthly activities of mobile phone users

Percent who do each activity on a cell phone/smartphone or
handheld wireless device at least monthly

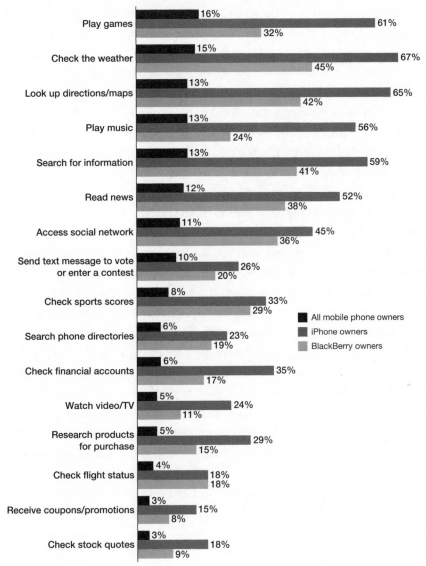

Base: U.S. online adults who have an active cell phone or smartphone.

Source: Forrester's North American Technographics Empowerment Online Survey, Q4 2009 (US).

a framework for mobile benefits

Before you go forward with a mobile application, you need to ask two basic questions: what's in it for your customers, and what's in it for you?

Remember that mobile applications are *voluntary*. Whether your application uses text messaging, a mobile Web site, or a dedicated application for a platform like the iPhone, your customers must choose to interact with it. You are competing not just with others in your industry, but with everything they can do on that phone right now.

Our analysis of successful mobile applications shows that the best empower customers with immediacy, simplicity, and context.[4] Immediacy means they deliver what the customer needs *right now*—whether it's a weather forecast, a list of local gay bars, or a stock quote for Cindie Parmelee. Simplicity is crucial because phones, even smartphones, have simple interfaces—they must deliver what the customers are seeking in a click or two, recognizing customers and taking advantage of the knowledge they've already shared with you. Context enhances the application's value by tapping into the phone's capability to know where they are, who their contacts are, and what they just took pictures of. Mobile phone owners are increasingly growing to expect this level of value, because mobile phone applications increasingly deliver it. So must you.

That's what's in it for customers. What's in it for you? Applications should increase sales, cut costs, increase loyalty, or otherwise benefit your business. They must be designed with these goals in mind. (We list some of these benefits in more detail in the next section.)

In general, the more useful or interesting your application is, the more people will use it. The more they use it, the more value they will get out of it. And the more value they find, the more positively inclined they will be toward your company. You can translate this into benefits. The key is to design a strategy that generates those benefits even as it delights your customers.

using the POST method to plan mobile strategy

The technological and strategic choices facing you as you deploy a mobile application are complex. You may be highly empowered and resourceful, but you still need a plan. We recommend that you follow the POST method, named for the four steps you follow in building your plan: *people, objectives, strategy, technology.* If you read *Groundswell,* you know we use the POST method for companies that are pursuing social technologies; the same basic technique applies in designing a mobile strategy. As with social applications, the key for mobile applications is to examine the people and objectives first, *before* designing a strategy and choosing a technology.[5]

people: examine your customers' mobile behaviors

Before you get started, evaluate the mobile behaviors of your target audience. Our survey research shows that E*TRADE's customers are nearly twice as likely to be connecting with the mobile Internet as average customers. This is the type of research E*TRADE used to decide that a BlackBerry application would be popular with its day traders and mass affluent customers.

As you can see from figure 5-1, owners of different types of mobile devices behave differently. And you need to plan not only for what devices and behaviors your customers have now, but for how their activities will change in the future. As a rule of thumb, younger customers are more comfortable with devices like the iPhone and mobile behaviors like texting and downloading content. And of course, in the United States and Europe, BlackBerry devices appeal more to professionals.

One quick way to assess your customers' profile is to look at the mobile browser traffic to your Web site. When Sears noticed increasing mobile traffic to its site, it designed a mobile Web site that delivered information to these customers better. Another retailer redesigned its mobile site after noting that 80 percent of the mobile traffic came from iPhones. If you've already got a mobile Web site, pay close attention to the devices that access it—this mix will tell you if it makes sense to create a mobile application for Apple, BlackBerry, or Google Android phones.

You can find out more with customer surveys or through information in syndicated surveys like Forrester's Technographics. Regardless of what method you use, though, don't design a mobile strategy until you've gathered intelligence about your customers' mobile behaviors.

objectives: determine how both you and your customers will benefit

Once you know your customers' mobile habits, you need to figure out why you're bothering to connect with them. Mobile applications can help with marketing, sales, and service; to be successful, you must narrow down which objective you're pursuing. There are three basic categories of mobile objective (and always remember, mobile offerings work only if your customers get as much out of them as you do).

INCREASING SALES. Mobile applications that increase sales succeed in multiple ways. For example, Pizza Hut's iPhone application generated more than $1 million in sales the first three months it was live. Targeting a young audience, Pizza Hut built a pizza delivery racing game into the app. Because the Pizza Hut app made it easy to add toppings, iPhone orders totaled significantly more per order than orders coming in by telephone calls.

You can also increase sales by increasing the information in interactions. Benjamin Moore's director of color technology, Carl Minchew, worked on the development of an iPhone app called ben Color Capture so customers could take photos and then find paint colors to match or complement colors in the photos. Inspiration like that can lead consumers from ideas to transactions.

Benjamin Moore's application also includes a store locator, a popular feature that helps drive sales. Target goes a step further on this front; its mobile application actually helps identify whether local stores have products in stock.

DECREASING COSTS. Mobile applications save money by connecting people directly with answers, removing service people from the process. This is a perfect example of a win-win, since the customer gets quicker service while the company saves costs and increases the quality of the interaction. Mobile connections are part of the groundswell customer service we described in the previous chapter.

For example, Nationwide Insurance built an iPhone app that walks its policyholders through the process of preparing to file a claim right at the scene of an auto accident.[6] The application includes prompts to take all the necessary steps, including calling the police, recording the location with GPS, taking photos, locating a repair shop, and even turning all the pixels white so the phone can be used as a flashlight. Customers get faster service and don't miss steps since they don't have to call an agent. Nationwide gets claims with more complete information, saving their claims agents time.

iPhone apps are not the only way to connect with customers. American Airlines delivers information on flights, delays, and cancellations with SMS, email, and a mobile site, the perfect way to reassure nervous travelers.

INCREASING LOYALTY. Even if you can't increase sales or decrease costs, mobile applications that supply information can generate love—or at least satisfaction. For example, Bank of America's online site and apps are designed to improve its customer experience. The apps are designed to answer questions like "Where is the closest ATM?" and "What's my balance?" The experience uses a login and authentication taken directly from the bank's online banking service, further reinforcing the idea that the company provides convenient service. Notice that these applications are not replacing calls—most of the inquiries conducted on mobile devices would never come into the bank as phone calls—but instead reinforcing the idea that the bank is a service leader. After 1 million iPhone downloads of the Bank of America app—the most of any financial application for the iPhone—the bank began publicizing its mobile phone services with TV commercials.

strategy: what's the long-term plan for your mobile application?

Once you've evaluated your people and objectives, refine your strategy. Remember the focus on immediacy, simplicity, and context, empowering customers with information. In this phase, you'll want to answer questions like these:

- Where will the information that fuels your application come from? What systems does your application need to touch and coordinate with (for example, billing, customer service, or your own Web group)?

- How will you publicize your application so customers know about it? Consider traditional advertising, customer emails, mobile services like AdMob, and signage.

- Once your application is built, will you concentrate on reaching more people by supporting more platforms, or on extending the functionality for the applications you have already built?

- How will you gather data from mobile users and use it to benefit your business? Who is responsible for that data?

- Is this a short-term promotion or a long-term commitment? If it's long-term, who will maintain the application?

- What's your model? Is the application actually a product you can charge for, or will you be delivering benefits to the rest of your business?

- How will you measure those benefits?

technology: what types of mobile application are you building?

Most people start their mobile thinking with technology, because the boss told them to build an iPhone app or his daughter is nuts about text messaging. It's far better to start by solidifying your people, objectives, and strategy. But eventually, you'll need to know how you'll deliver mobile value. Your strategy can include one or more of the following:

- *Text messaging.* Messaging strategies have the enormous benefit that nearly every phone supports them, and over half of U.S. mobile phone users use text messages. Text messages, also known as SMS (short message service), are suited to the timely delivery of perishable information, like eBay auctions; query responses, like stock quotes; and voting and sweepstakes entries.

- *Mobile sites.* At this writing, one in nine mobile phone customers say they access the Web monthly on their phones; we expect this to grow to 39 percent by 2014. Reconfiguring your site to recognize and deliver content for mobile phones makes sense, but it's far more than just shoving content around. You'll need to identify which bits of information are most valuable to mobile users and design layouts, menus, and graphics to deliver them quickly. The emerging Web standard HTML5 will make mobile sites easier to create.

- *Apps.* Since the iPhone came out, apps are all the rage. While apps can get access to phone features like location, the camera, messaging, and links to other Web sites, they can cost around $100,000 to develop. Since they take a moment for customers to download and take up space on the phone's display, you'll need to spend money to promote them to generate awareness and make sure they have value. Another challenge is the variety of incompatible app platforms from Apple, Google, RIM, and others.

Amid this broad landscape of choices, successful companies stand out for the innovative ways they are delighting their customers. We'll highlight two: a support application for stadium events and an iPhone app for the shipping company UPS.

CASE STUDY

help! i'm in a stadium full of football fans and i have a problem

There's really nothing quite like sitting in a stadium watching an elite professional sports team like the NFL's Philadelphia Eagles compete. To be right there, in the out-of-doors along with tens of thousands of fellow Eagles fans, is incomparable. It's not cheap, but it's a unique entertainment experience that's worth the price. Assuming nothing goes wrong, that is.

Leonard Bonacci, director of event operations for the Eagles, is responsible for the fan experience at Lincoln Financial Field, home field for the Eagles, Temple University, and other events including concerts and soccer games. For every home game, around sixty-eight thousand people are expecting to have that incomparable experience.

Leonard's challenge is the disruptive fan. He and his staff of a few dozen must monitor 1.7 million square feet of stadium with their eyes and ears, closed-circuit TV feeds, and binoculars. Things go wrong.

People throw up on seats. A guy starts shouting obscenities at the top of his lungs for fifteen minutes straight. Leonard's staff can't be everywhere at once, and people are often unwilling to interrupt their game experience to get security. So for each disruptive fan, a few others might leave the game annoyed, wondering if it was worth it.

At least that's how it was until Leonard implemented GuestAssist, a text-messaging system. It's simple. Tickets and signs on the back of seats tell fans with a problem to send a text message to a five-digit short-code with their location and a request for help. The messages show up on a central console; Leonard and his staff can rapidly send people in to help. For example, "Drunk guy passed out in my seat in section 110." Or (and yes, this is a real example) "The person wearing the birthday cake hat in front of me is blocking my view." The messages are anonymous and discreet—the offender doesn't know who's complaining. As Leonard says, "It adds sixty-eight thousand security guards to your operation." The system works because nearly everyone in the stadium has a mobile phone and most know how to text.

Despite the ease of use of the system, only a few hundred messages get sent each season, few enough that they're far more likely to help with satisfaction than to overwhelm the staff. Sure, they have to ignore the occasional irrelevant message (one fed-up fan texted "Help, the offense has been stolen") but texting back "Please use this only for emergency purposes" typically shuts down that sort of activity. As a result of the text-messaging system, Eagles surveys show fan satisfaction has significantly increased.

Leonard Bonacci, who started as a stadium worker in 1997, proved he was a highly empowered and resourceful operative by pioneering in-stadium text messaging in the NFL. The changes he brought to Philadelphia in 2007 spread. Two years later, the NFL has made what the Eagles were doing a leaguewide best practice. GuestAssist and a competitor, In-Stadium Services, now provide text-messaging help services at every NFL stadium, along with hundreds of other arenas around the country, including college stadiums. Stadium security can't stop people from getting drunk or unruly, but with text messaging, they can ensure everyone with a phone can report a problem, making it easier to improve the value fans get for their money.

use text messaging for reach

As the Eagles' fan-support application proves, you don't need to build an app to take advantage of mobile connections. While text-messaging applications can serve a variety of objectives, they have one thing in common—they're designed to have the broadest reach possible.

On the other hand, text-messaging applications don't allow for deep interactions. The key word for text messages is *notification*. You can use them to notify customers of anything from marketing messages to bank balances. And customers can use them to notify *you* of problems or needs, as the Eagles' fans do.

If your main objective is support, then delivering text messages as a service can help create loyalty. This is why so many airlines enable text messaging for flight updates. The Weather Channel/weather.com reinforces its image as the leading supplier of weather information by enabling customers to sign up for text message weather alerts. Should you pursue these types of support applications? Yes, if (1) your customers typically need information on the go, when they're not at a computer and (2) they'll associate your updates with real value from your company. But remember that information exchanged in this way must be very short and simple; if you desire more complex interactions, you're better off with a full mobile site or application.

A final note on text-messaging applications: they may catch on more broadly in countries where smartphones and broadband are less popular. In India, where far more people have mobile phones than computers and broadband connections, a company called SMS GupShup has set up a community program through mobile phone text messaging. (GupShup roughly translates as "chit chat.") Customers can create or follow groups for anything (local events, jokes, foods, politics), and messages sent to these groups are shared with all followers. Since its launch in 2007, GupShup has attracted 30 million members and grown to 5 percent of all the text message traffic in India, where it occupies a niche similar to Twitter. GupShup works with marketers; for example, UTI, a mutual fund company, started a mobile community to engage with its four hundred forty thousand existing customers; their text-message referrals helped UTI to acquire an additional thirty-nine thousand community members. Among other services, this system automatically responds to text messages seeking the location of local UTI branches.

For many marketers and their customers, though, text messages and mobile Web sites aren't sufficiently empowering. These companies deliver service and information through apps, like UPS.

CASE STUDY

why UPS must deliver a full mobile experience

UPS is the world's largest shipping company, delivering 15 million packages every day;[7] in the United States, those deliveries account for 6 percent of the nation's global domestic product. Technology is central to the business, and its customers depend on those connections. Every day its Web site, UPS.com, gets 20.4 million page views and answers 22.4 million tracking requests. UPS knows where every package is, but just as important for its business, that information infrastructure is accessible—once you send a package, *you* can know where it is at any moment you care to ask.

Given the global competition for package services, the company must empower customers to connect with it in any way they want. That's why the company has over forty-six hundred UPS store outlets and over forty thousand drop boxes. And it's why, if people have smart-phones, including iPhones, UPS must be on those devices.

In October 2009, UPS released the UPS Mobile App for the iPhone after two months of development. According to Jordan Colletta, vice president of customer technology marketing at UPS, the purpose of the iPhone app is simple: to deliver all the functionality that customers get at UPS.com, but on their iPhone. This includes not just tracking packages but shipping; the app makes it easy to input information for a package, and sends the label to any email address where you can print it out. If you're already a UPS customer, the app has access to your UPS address book and preferences.

UPS had to go mobile. "Our goal is to make UPS accessible 24/7 in processes that customers do all the time. We don't view our mobile apps as separate, we view them as an extension of our capabilities at UPS.com," says Jordan.

Based on the traffic to UPS's mobile Web site, m.ups.com, the company had a good idea of what to expect and what to build. Some customers on the mobile site were frustrated they could only track packages, not arrange for shipping; the app needed to include shipping. The Web interactions needed a redesign to eliminate steps and clicks, boosting simplicity and immediacy. The strength of the application was in the cloud: UPS's worldwide collection of servers that knew every customer's information and could make it available to that customer on any connected device.[8]

UPS's iPhone app was a clear success, with two hundred thousand downloads in the first two months, catapulting it into position as one of the top three business apps within days of its release. Shipments through the iPhone were higher than the company expected from the previous traffic to the mobile site; apparently having an app in the palm of your hand gets customers shipping. The company had to be on the iPhone, and they had to get the experience right. UPS has since added an app for the BlackBerry and upgraded its mobile Web site to include shipping. Why? Because the company had already set expectations of instant accessibility both online and in its stores. UPS had to meet those expectations on the device that people carry with them everywhere—their phone.

app strategy

With apps for the iPhone climbing into the hundreds of thousands, companies are stampeding into the app store. Before you join the stampede, ask a few questions:

- *Are your customers there?* iPhones and other smartphones generally reach young, technology-ready business customers. If these are your customers, go forward; if not, you might want to rethink your app strategy. Check how much of your Web site's traffic comes from mobile devices now to get a good idea of the potential level of demand.

- *What information do your customers need on the go?* If you're UPS or E*TRADE, that information is similar to what's on your Web site. But if you're a packaged goods or retail company, you may need to think a little harder; another store locator isn't likely to attract a huge audience. Kraft's iFood Assistant app became one of the top hundred apps by making it easy for people to choose from seven thousand recipes by type or even by available ingredients—perfect when you're panicked and forty-five minutes from dinner. (And of course, the recipes feature Kraft products.) Like Kraft, you may have to use your imagination to identify how you can best help your customers—and yourself—when they're away from the computer.

- *What phone features can you benefit from?* NIKEiD, an application in which customers can order color-customized Nike shoes, encourages customers to use the phone's camera to capture colors, then suggests shoes that others have ordered that feature those colors. Urban Spoon uses the phone's GPS locator and compass to superimpose restaurant names and ratings over the view from the camera. Stanley uses the phone's accelerometer to turn the phone into a level. These apps unmistakably demonstrate a cool factor by taking advantage of the phone, and will attract customers by making their phones more useful. Using phone features in a unique way makes it likely that you'll attract more customers, and that they'll buzz about the app, generating additional downloads.

- *What's your long-term platform plan?* Most of the companies we spoke with, including UPS and E*TRADE, planned to be on multiple phone platforms moving forward. Unless your customers are BlackBerry zealots or iPhone purists, you'll probably need to tread this path as well, at least until standards like HTML5 allow for common development for different phones. Regardless, you should build the architecture of your application—and the information sources it connects to—in such a way that you can easily construct interfaces when the next hot phone comes out. This is harder than it sounds, because phone features and screen sizes vary.

- *What resources will maintain your application?* An app is like a Web site; it needs attention in the short term to fix bugs (new versions of the iPhone software often require small revisions) and over time, to keep up with new technologies. If your application is clearly a short-term one-shot (a name like "2012 Olympic athlete tracker" would be one clue), you'll still need to plan on how to sunset it when its value runs out.

- *What's your promotional strategy?* You need a way to get the app into the hands of the customers. If you end up near the top of the charts like UPS's and Kraft's apps, people will find you just by searching the app store, but as the flood of apps becomes a torrent, planning to be in that position is like planning to write a bestseller—it's a strategy at which 98 percent will fail. Instead, consider using mobile ad platforms like AdMob, tags on TV and print ads, customer emails, PR, and other forms of outbound communication to get your app talked about. And if possible, find ways in which those who love the app can easily share their feelings though social technologies like Twitter and Facebook.

global mobile strategy

Web strategy tends to be fairly standard across geographies. But if you're a multinational company pursuing mobile strategies, you've got challenges. Everything varies by country—the types of handsets available, the way operators charge for mobile downloads, even the prevalence and usage models for text messaging. In some developing countries, the mobile phone is becoming the primary interactive platform. These habits change the ways people interact and set their expectations; they're why mobile social networking in the United States is most likely to be a Twitter or Facebook app, while social networking in India happens through SMS GupShup and text messaging.

To manage this diversity, start by picking the countries or regions you want to target and choosing appropriate types of applications for the usage models in those countries. If you pursue several geographies, look for commonalities in platforms, strategy, promotion, or application architecture. Different countries may end up leading based both on local cultural readiness and the initiative of HEROes in different geographies.

For large multinational companies, the best way to manage this may be through a council of global mobile application managers who meet and share best practices (we describe councils of this kind in chapter 9).

the risks of not doing a mobile application

As you look at the complexity of mobile strategy, you may be tempted to give up and stick with what you know—online or social applications, for example.

Don't give up so easily, though.

Given the interactive capabilities of mobile devices, the kind of people who have them, and the incredible features they offer, it's likely that mobile connections will outpace other online connections in coming years. When your customers went online in the 1990s, you followed them there. Now that they're mobile in the 2010s, you'll need to empower them there as well.

Keep in mind as well that the most active mobile customers are the same empowered consumers to whom you want to deliver the best service. Your mobile customer is likely to look like Maytag customer Heather Armstrong or United flier Dave Carroll. If these people love you, they'll spread that love. If they don't, your other customers will hear about it from them. So keep them happy with a solid, valuable, loyalty-generating mobile application, and give them every reason to tell their friends.

getting happy customers talking

Now you've seen three of the elements of the empowered-consumer IDEA—identifying mass influencers, delivering groundswell customer service, and empowering customers with mobile information. What's left? Taking the fans you've identified and energized and amplifying their voices. Chapter 6 describes the techniques for doing this, not just with a few loudmouths, but with masses of customers.

6. amplifying your fans

You just experienced one of the most visible and disappointing product launches in history. Your main competitor has a burgeoning cool factor and makes fun of you—quite believably—in its commercials. Is this the time to start a social technology campaign?

If you're Microsoft, it is.

In 2008, Microsoft's Windows marketing was picking itself up off the mat. Despite the challenging and frustrating launch of Windows Vista, the company still had quite a few assets. When you have a ninety-plus-percent market share, there are a lot of people who use and like your product. The company decided to find those fans and get its mojo back.

One of the first things Marty Collins did when she became community manager for Windows in July 2008 was to create a YouTube channel soliciting customer videos on the theme "I'm a PC," the very words delivered by the nerdy PC character in Apple's ubiquitous commercials. Sure enough, thousands of videos poured in. Based on this response, Microsoft edited them together in short snippets to create a series of "I'm a PC" commercials.[1] This was the beginning of the Windows brand's resurgence—and proof that fans were a key to Windows marketing success. As Marty described it, "We have a very strong competitor, and it has a very strong fan base. We know that a lot of times our enthusiasts will not be the loudest voice in a conversation . . . We created a groundswell of people that finally said, 'I love this machine, I love this operating system.'"

This success in hand, the Windows team geared up for the launch of Windows 7. The prerelease beta version launched in January 2009. Using Trucast, a Web monitoring product from Visible Technologies, the community team monitored the reactions to the beta version on blogs, discussion forums, Twitter, and elsewhere. Based on online social commentary, people perceived Windows 7 as a "vast improvement." And Marty knew that amplifying this sentiment would help accelerate the launch, planned for October. So she and her colleagues at Microsoft did three things.

First, Marty's team collected a moderated feed of all the social posts about Windows 7 from Twitter, Facebook, blogs, YouTube, and Flickr into one highly dynamic site[2] at www.windows.com/social. The site accumulated over three hundred thousand posts in the first five months after launch. Microsoft featured this feed on various social sites, like its Facebook page, and during the week of the Windows 7 launch, right on the Windows.com home page. Why? Because people's voluntary, authentic, and even misspelled comments are more persuasive than a bunch of polished but hard-to-credit material that Microsoft wants to promote.

Second, the advertising team took its cues from the successful "I'm a PC" campaign and during the launch ran customer-centered television, print, and outdoor advertising focused on customer suggestions. The new campaign centered around the tagline "I'm a PC, and Windows 7 was my idea," with specific examples of features suggested by PC owners, like faster start-up. With this campaign, Microsoft reinforced the idea that it had listened to customers in the time since Vista was released and had improved the product. This campaign was credible, in part, because of all the authentic customer activity that the company was sharing.

Finally, Microsoft found a very immediate way to get masses of its actual fans to share their enthusiasm. If you were a Windows 7 fan you could sign up to have a party in your home to show off the new features—Microsoft would send along materials, including a special prerelease Windows 7 disk signed by Steve Ballmer. (House Party, a company that creates in-home word-of-mouth programs, managed this project.) Word about the party opportunities spread through social media and before long, tens of thousands of people in fourteen different countries had signed up. Microsoft estimates that the parties reached about eight hundred thousand people, including hosts and guests. Many contributed comments like this to the company's party central site:

> Everyone had a great time! . . . People loved how easy it was to use Windows 7 and the fact it was so easy to stream movies to the X box 360. They loved my dad's homemade pizza and Dairy Queens Windows 7 ice cream cake.

Hundreds of thousands of party attendees were highly engaged with the new operating system. Research confirmed that people who had been to the parties had moved forward on the key awareness and engagement metrics that Microsoft tracks for marketing.

The success of the parties came with one unexpected result. House Party had created a video to train party hosts—a video with an ethnically mixed set of "typical" partygoers that comes off, shall we say, a little stilted and square.[3] Perfect for a brand that has embraced its inner nerd. It was easy to make fun of and generated widespread ridicule. But for the same reason, it was easy to spread. The video went viral on YouTube, where it has been viewed over one million times. That's a million people paying attention to Windows 7 features for six minutes, even as they mock Microsoft's marketing. But that's fine with the Windows team, since they've realized that their fans know as much about how to market the new operating system as they do.

the truth about word-of-mouth marketing

Does *your* product have fans?

If you're Jeep or Apple or the Boston Red Sox, of course you do. But even if you're not, there are plenty of people using your product. They like some things about you. You have good design, a good price, or good service. Or you're close by and quick. You may not have fans like the Boston Red Sox (after all, Red Sox fans by the hundreds go to away games in Baltimore just to see them play), but you *do* have people willing to say nice things about you, your company, your products, and your services.

Now you can see where this fits in with the last three chapters. Remember the first three steps in IDEA: first, identify the type of people who like and talk about your products; second, deliver groundswell customer service to create more happy customers; and third, empower them with mobile information. Those activities help you identify a large enough pool of people who will potentially like you enough to talk. Energizing those fans, and amplifying their conversation is the payoff.

This is exactly what Marty Collins and Microsoft did. While less than 2 percent of the online population are Mass Connectors for PCs and software and less than 5 percent are Mass Mavens, this is still millions of people, and most of them use PCs. Our research shows that this group likes to talk on the channels that the windows.com/social site was amplifying: Facebook, Twitter, and blogs.

If you want to make that word of mouth work for you as it did for Microsoft, you'll need to keep two things in mind.

First, the term *word-of-mouth marketing,* while very popular right now, is misleading. The reason: marketers generally work in terms of campaigns with a starting point and an endpoint, while word-of-mouth activities go on and on. Microsoft's Marty Collins took the approach that the fan base could be nurtured over time. She gave them a platform and a way to persuade others. Microsoft's house parties and advertising may have been timed to energize them during the Windows 7 launch, but Marty and Microsoft continue to cultivate their fan base.

This is hard for marketers. Fan bases take time to build. If you have as many customers as Microsoft, you can get a critical mass going in months; if your customer base is smaller, it will take longer. In any case, you'll be out of sync with short-term-focused marketing efforts like advertising.

Instead, think of fan base cultivation as building an asset over time, in the same way you think about brand building. This means that when your fan program has done its work—when the product is launched or the campaign is over—you don't throw those fans on the scrap heap. You cultivate them, since you'll need them next time. Like customer service, fan base cultivation is an activity that never ends.[4]

The second thing to keep in mind is that fan programs must be run efficiently. This is not PR outreach to influential journalists and bloggers—that sort of program needs to be run with individual attention. And it's not mass marketing either, in which you bombard your whole customer base with messages. Instead, it's an appeal to the mass influencers we defined in chapter 3. The trick in fan marketing is to unlock the power of individuals to influence their friends, colleagues, and followers with an efficient mass program.

In this chapter, we'll show several cases and examples of word-of-mouth marketing programs that worked for both long-term value and efficiency. But to get started with a program of this kind, you'll have to take it one step at a time.

five steps for fan marketing

Why is marketing with fans harder than it seems? Because at a lot of companies, marketing's main job is to turn noncustomers into customers. Once they're customers, they go into customer service, which focuses on retention. But retention is not enough. Given the potency of empowered customers, marketing needs to focus on them every bit as much as the service department does.

Having acquired a bunch of customers, you should be doing everything possible to maintain a connection with them. You should develop a healthy obsession with what they are talking about, whom they are talking to, and what they want. Only then can you determine how best to encourage them to speak about your products.

And as Microsoft found out, what they want to talk about and where may not match up to what your marketing thinks is best. Smart companies seeing this don't give up on word of mouth or try to fit it into a mold. *They change their marketing.* They may even change their products. The word of mouth of your customers is a gift. Embrace it.

Focusing much of your marketing on current customers will feel fundamentally weird to most marketers. Since you started your career, you've been trained to focus on reaching new customers and on generating awareness. As for outreach to existing customers, the main focus was typically to get repeat business.

To get your head in the right place, start with this: imagine for a moment that the only way you could get awareness, create interest, and generate a sale was to persuade an existing customer to promote your product. What would you do? This is the new mind-set—a mind-set that embraces empowered customers. This is the five-step method for amplifying word of mouth:

1. *Outside perspective.* Build systems and dedicate resources to collecting and analyzing customer perspectives.

2. *Respond.* Create identities in the places your customers go and reach out to them.

3. *Enable.* Give your customers tools, content, and opportunities to talk about you.

4. *Amplify.* Find ways to connect fans to each other, and to the rest of the world.

5. *Change.* Help your company learn from fan activity and become better.

As you start on this journey, know that you'll likely be taking all five steps. Listening to the outside perspective stimulates responses, which takes you deeper into enabling and amplifying your fans. And once you're engaged with those fans, they *will* influence and change your company.

outside perspective: develop the discipline of listening

Conversing with customers is terrifying for marketers. That's why most companies don't do it. Marketing creates constructs like "target markets" with neat statistical work. Sure, you do focus groups, but you stay on the other side of that one-way glass. Having been paid, focus group participants are usually civil. In contrast, there are no inhibitions online—people can say *anything*.

What a valuable resource—real frank discussion.

The fear of engaging with customers usually springs from ignorance. Ignorance is curable. Cure it. Start listening.

Begin by analyzing where your customers are talking to each other. Is Facebook more important, or should you concentrate on discussion forums? One way to figure this out is with a peer influence analysis of your market—you can check out the ones in chapter 3 for some guidance.

Then see what people are saying. Choose a listening platform—a company that, for a fee, will help you monitor online commentary about your company and your products.[5] Radian6 may be the most economical; others include TNS Cymfony, Nielsen Buzzmetrics, and Sysomos. Since fan marketing requires you to wade into and amplify this conversation, you'd better understand it first.

Here's an example of how one organization turned that outside perspective into value. McNally Smith College of Music in St. Paul, Minnesota, wanted to differentiate itself from larger and better-known music colleges. It hired a company called Risdall Marketing Group to analyze online conversations around music colleges. Risdall's analysis of online monitoring reports from Radian6 indicated the key topics of conversation. Only after this step was complete could McNally Smith plunge in, connect with the people talking about music colleges, and become part of the conversation. Before this program, McNally Smith was mentioned in 2.7 percent of online conversations about music colleges; afterward, it was mentioned in 12.1 percent.[6]

This example shows two things: first, listening is not enough, you must engage to make an impact. And second, you have to keep listening to see if it's working. But like McNally Smith, you'll find that listening gets you familiar with what's being said and where; it's the first step to energizing fans.

respond: connect with customers

Listening in groundswell channels generates the urge to participate. Go ahead, connect with your customers. But too many marketers treat these channels as a checklist. It's true, you ought to be in Twitter, on

Facebook, commenting on blogs, and participating in discussion forums—your analysis gained through the outside perspective stage can tell you how to prioritize these channels.

But your presence needs to be part of a strategy to respond to others and create opportunities for others to respond to you. You should be able to (1) respond to requests for service or information (because once you appear, customers will expect this); (2) make marketing announcements (but be careful, a little of this goes a long way), and (3) engage fans with content that excites them (this is the core of fan marketing).

To do this properly, you'll need a dedicated resource to staff this channel. That person must be able to make customer service connections, not just speak for marketing; your customers will expect it. The person operating the accounts must be able to respond quickly without authorization; a better policy is to set guidelines in advance so she can work within them.

Finally, remember that your objective here is to encourage fans. So start making notes of who's talking about you (Twitter handles, blogs, forum participants) and get ready to reach out to them more directly. In this context, you'll often find that people whose problem you've solved are the most enthusiastic, because your outreach changed them from detractors to promoters.

enable: make it easy to share

You've identified where your customers are talking and what they're saying. You've got people in your own organization in position and responding. Only now can you get started on the effective work in fan marketing—making it easier for fans who like you to talk about you.

Your job is simply to shorten the distance between a happy customer and an encouraging comment. Here are some ways to do that:

- *Create graphics and other shareable elements for use in Facebook, MySpace, Twitter, and other social environments.* One of the most innovative applications of this kind that we've seen is the one created by AMC for the TV series *Mad Men*.[7] Over seven hundred thousand visitors used this Web application to create an avatar of themselves, sized perfectly for Twitter. By allowing *Mad Men* fans to demonstrate their love, the program's reach and cool factor went up, generating mainstream press notices in places like the *Boston Herald* and leading to a third season premiere that earned a 273 percent ratings increase over the previous year.

- *Encourage existing fans.* How do you react when your fans promote your brand? You could sue them for copyright violations. Or you could embrace them and supply them with the tools they need to keep promoting you. Coca-Cola did this well when it reached out to Dusty Sorg and Michael Jedrzejewski, two fans who ran the most popular of more than two hundred fifty Coca-Cola fan pages on Facebook.[8] Rather than sue them or compete with them, Coca-Cola proposed to help them run the page. By collaborating with its fans on the page, Coca-Cola garnered 3 million fans, making it the second most popular fan page on Facebook (after Barack Obama).

- *Participate in discussion forums.* Even companies that build their own support forums will often find their products and services discussed elsewhere. Forum members are often grateful when companies participate in a helpful way, offering links to their own materials and content. This works far better than ham-handed attempts to promote yourself. Be careful to obey the terms and conditions of the community, which typically prohibit bald promotional efforts.

- *Start or encourage a viral campaign.* While fan activity is often self-generating, you can also create opportunities for fans to spread your messages. The simplest way to do this is with a video, like Evian's video featuring break-dancing babies on roller skates.[9] This sixty-second spot is so silly and exuberant that 12 million people have viewed it in six months. Countless others have embedded it in blogs and elsewhere; for example, one hundred seventy thousand views came from Facebook.

amplify: connect customers with one another

If you publish a book, you can put a few good review quotes on the back. The ad for your movie can tell viewers that the *New York Times* called it a "must-see."

But in the groundswell, every comment can be recycled. Social applications make it far easier to identify reviews and put them in places where others can see them.

We call this step "amplify" since it takes existing word of mouth and pumps up the volume. When Microsoft's Marty Collins put the social comments about Windows 7 on the Windows home page, she vastly increased the reach of these comments. Where a person's comment may have had ten or a hundred followers, she put it in front of tens of thousands. This is the step that makes fan marketing worthwhile by increasing the reach of messages.

Sonic Foundry, a technology vendor that sells Webcasts to corporations, is one company that turned this sort of concentration of messages to its advantage.[10] Travel bans and the economic downturn of 2009 had dented the company's prospects for its annual user conference in Madison, Wisconsin, an event that normally generated a lot of business. Sonic Foundry took advantage of its strength with video to record and broadcast interviews with members at the conference, and to Webcast the entire event. By featuring users (and retweeting their tweets), the company spread the enthusiasm of a live event to many who weren't there in person. As a result, Sonic Foundry saw a 15 percent increase in paying conference attendees, of whom 10 percent were attending virtually over the Net.

Another way to amplify word of mouth is to make customer reviews easier to write and publish. Diane Beaudet, senior director of user engagement for the antivirus and security programs from Symantec's Norton division, knew she had customers who loved the product—she could see them talking about it on Facebook and Twitter. But on sites featuring ratings and reviews, Norton's ratings were decidedly mixed. Working with Zuberance, a word-of-mouth marketing company, Norton put a one-question survey in front of people visiting its Web site. Those who said they would recommend the Norton brand to others were invited to join a program called Norton Advocates. Zuberance helped Norton Advocates members to write and publish reviews on sites like Amazon and CNET. As a result, in a short time, Norton's average ratings on those sites went from two stars to four and a half (on a five-point scale).[11]

Amplifying has its challenges. In the case of Norton and Zuberance, some Norton Advocates members were at first rewarded with redeemable "points" for sharing promotions, but the companies quickly discontinued that element of the program to avoid the appearance that incentives were driving participation. Microsoft moderates the comments that appear on its Windows Social page to ensure that offensive material is not passed through. Some social technology experts, like Sam Decker, head of marketing for the social commerce technology vendor Bazaarvoice, counsel marketers to maintain authenticity in sourcing customer content.[12] He suggests asking whether you'd be comfortable revealing how you solicited these sorts of reviews and comments. Our view: marketers must be very careful about cherry-picking or skewing social activity that they amplify. In the case of Norton and Zuberance, for example, while the customers encouraged to submit reviews were those who were favorably inclined toward the product, the company simply led the reviewers to the doorstep of the sites and allowed them to type whatever they wanted.

Can amplifying backfire? Of course. On March 2, 2009, the candy brand Skittles replaced its home page skittles.com with feeds from social media—Tweets about Skittles, YouTube videos about Skittles, and so on. Unlike Microsoft's efforts, there was very little moderation. On the plus side, the site saw a 1,332 percent increase in Web visitors, driven by news coverage, word of mouth, and curiosity.[13] Of course, a lot of the activity devolved into "Look, I can tweet about Skittles and get the F-word onto their home page." We found this stunt lacking, because brand fans were quickly overwhelmed by fame seekers.

Regardless of what techniques you use, here's what happens when you complete the first four steps of fan marketing: you learn a lot about your customers. "Respond" doesn't just mean helping them—it means respecting their desires for change. And this leads to the fifth step of fan marketing—changing your company.

change: revise your marketing and your products

Marketing is about resonance. Good marketers seek ideas about what resonates with customers. That's one of the best things about fan marketing—you learn what resonates. Nearly every marketer we spoke with for this chapter told us that they were changing their marketing based on insights from customers.

Take Swarovski, an Austrian company that makes small gemstones used in jewelry, including watches. Among its main marketing tools are brochures used at jewelry shows, intended to give jewelry manufacturers ideas about how to incorporate the Swarovski gems into their designs. The company conducted an online contest for watch designs in 2008, attracting more than nine hundred innovative designs.[14] The company selected the best of these and created its marketing brochure from them. If jewelry manufacturers like a design in the brochure, they contact the original designer. With this innovative program, the company has turned watch designers into Swarovski promoters, given its manufacturing customers access to a new source of creativity, and boosted the visibility of its gemstone products.

Companies are beginning to realize that empowered customers are a great source of innovative ideas. The Starbucks site mystarbucks idea.com has now generated over eighty thousand ideas for the company, of which over fifty have been implemented.[15] Intuit has recruited seventeen thousand people into its TurboTax Inner Circle; the company uses them as a sounding board for new tax preparation software ideas.[16] And the auto-racing organization NASCAR, taking cues from its twelve-thousand-member fan community, changed the rules for races;[17] now, in a restart after a yellow caution flag, the cars start double file instead of single file. The fans love it.

Companies like to imagine they "control" their brands, but with empowered customers ready at any moment to hijack your brand identity, that concept is in danger. Embracing and amplifying the voices of your fans is one way to ally yourself with empowered customers. Just be aware that once you've taken this step, customers will be influencing your marketing and design decisions.

We'll demonstrate some of these ideas with two more case studies that show the range of companies that can use fan marketing. One example comes from sports, where fans are central to everything. The other comes from pharmaceuticals, a regulated industry that requires a little more careful thinking to tap into word of mouth.

CASE STUDY

the NHL turns tweets into fan enthusiasm

Dani Muccio didn't grow to appreciate hockey until her three sons began to play. As she watched them skate around the rink—and watched some professional players from the New York Islanders skate at camps her kids attended—she began to see the beauty of the game her husband had been trying to get her interested in for years.

Dani wanted to connect with other people who felt the same way about hockey as she did. Her idea crystallized when she attended a tweetup—an in-person meeting of Twitter members who share a common interest. Her first tweetup wasn't about hockey, but she vowed her next one would be.

"Hockey is the red-headed stepchild of the sports world," Dani explains. Football and baseball fans are everywhere; hockey fans need to work a bit harder to find each other. A tweetup would afford them a way to connect. So Dani started tweeting about her idea, using the hashtag #NHLTweetup.[18] (Since a hashtag is a searchable term that people include in tweets, Dani knew other fans could go to search.twit ter.com and search on "NHLTweetup" to find other tweets on the topic.)

Mike DiLorenzo was the director of corporate communications for the NHL at the time. He was concerned about what happens every year as the hockey playoffs begin. "Hockey fans are very tribal," he says. At the start of the playoffs, fourteen of the thirty teams have already been eliminated. His challenge was to find ways to get fans of teams that did not qualify for the playoffs—the New York Islanders and

Nashville Predators, for example—to watch games between other play-off teams. So when he saw Dani's tweets about NHL tweetups, he knew her idea could be the spark he needed.

The first NHL tweetup was held in the NHL store in midtown Manhattan. The NHL provided the venue and included some souvenirs like signed NHL jerseys and an autographed guitar donated by Gibson. Dani got a friend to put up a Web site. Dani, Mike, and other tweeters they knew spread the word and generated the excitement. And the NHL lined up some of its sponsors: Bud Light to supply the beer and McDonald's to deliver the food. There's nothing like a fan to start a movement. Two hundred people showed up for the tweetup, but the impact was far greater. On the day of the tweetup, #NHLTweetup was the top trending topic on Twitter—meaning it was the most popular new topic being discussed by Twitter members. (This is like a book hitting the bestseller list—millions of Twitter members view the trending topics and then search them to see what people are talking about.) The people who came to the tweetup tweeted from their mobile phones while they were at the party. According to *USA Today*, the people at the New York tweetup had 21,336 followers, all of whom could be hearing about the hockey happening in New York, in real time.[19]

The NHL Tweetups continued in twenty-two other locations. One hundred people showed up in Nashville, even without free food. Three hundred and fifty showed up in Regina, Saskatchewan, which doesn't even have an NHL team. Two got together in London. To test the effects of all this activity, Mike included coupons in the gift bags that went out to the local tweetups. Result: thousands of purchases and tens of thousands of dollars of merchandise sold at Shop.NHL.com.

The NHL has now created a social media department and put Mike in charge of it. Mike believes the tweetups improved hockey's playoff ratings, and the NHL now has 355,000 followers on Twitter. Dani continues to coordinate the tweetups—it's a labor of love for her, all volunteer work—and Mike is too smart to mess with fans on a mission. "My discovery," he says, "is that social networks are not about Web sites . . . they are about creating or enhancing experiences for our fans."

lessons from fans

You may think that sports doesn't have much in common with your business. We're betting it does. The NHL has a core group of avid fans of its product, many more who are casually interested, and an even larger group of potential fans who don't care (yet). Isn't it the same for your company?

In terms of the five-step process for amplifying word of mouth, Mike DiLorenzo learned about Dani through Twitter (outside perspective), connected with her (respond), created a place and merchandise for the New York tweetup (enable), and used the NHL Twitter account to connect others with NHLTweetup.com (amplify). With Mike now in charge of social media for the NHL, the league is likely to rethink how it markets itself based on all the social activity. When social gets into a company, the last step, change, will happen.

Fans can say just about anything about sports, and the leagues love it. Contrast this free-for-all environment with what happens in a regulated industry like financial services or pharmaceuticals. Can fan marketing work there? Yes, but you'll have to be a little more careful.

CASE STUDY

finding fans for pharmaceuticals

You probably have no idea how paranoid drug companies are about following the rules from regulatory bodies like the U.S. Food and Drug Administration (FDA). Fines can run to billions of dollars. Our report about using social media in the pharmaceutical industry was titled "How To Create A Social Application For Life Sciences Without Getting Fired."[20] And it was aptly named, as it turned out—one marketer told me she would lose her job if I published a description of her application, even though it had been announced publicly.

So we were surprised to see that some life sciences companies were not only creating successful fan marketing programs, but doing very well with them. It's all a matter of following the rules very carefully.

Think about it. If you're miserable because of some disease or condition and a medical product makes things better, you're going to want to share. The drug company can't just create an unmoderated discussion forum and invite you to participate—you might recommend some inappropriate usage model, or fail to disclose side effects, which are exactly the activities the FDA punishes. But if you obey a few rules, the company can help you talk about your success.

People who suffer arthritic knee problems are a great example. Not only are they in agony, they worry that they're headed down the road to knee-replacement surgery. But Genzyme makes a product called Synvisc-One that can help. It's an artificial lubricant, injected into the knee joint once every six months. I (Josh) had heard of this product because it enabled my father, a lifelong tennis player, to continue to play at age seventy-seven. For the people it helps, it's a godsend.

Christine Waite, the associate director of consumer marketing at Genzyme, knew that this word of mouth was waiting to be unlocked—she'd done surveys that showed that 80 percent of Synvisc-One customers were ready to recommend the product. Her problem was straightforward: awareness of Synvisc-One is low among the patients who need it, typically people fifty-five and older. (Also, Synvisc is hard to spell, which challenges people doing Web searches.)

Anyone interested in nonstandard forms of marketing in the pharmaceutical industry is a HERO, because you have to be both empowered and resourceful to get the lawyers and regulatory affairs people to okay your program. The resource Christine needed to get Synvisc-One fans talking was Andrew Levitt, the founder of HealthTalker, a company dedicated to spreading fan word of mouth for life sciences companies.

They started by emailing to a small subset of Genzyme's database of about a hundred thousand people who have had Synvisc-One treatments or asked about it, directing people to a survey. The survey identified people who would be willing to tell others about it. Genzyme designed the invitation so that for this pilot project only a small group—four hundred fifty—of the most enthusiastic Synvisc-One fans would qualify.

Christine's HealthTalker program directed these patients/fans to kneeconnections.com, a site where they registered and filled out a profile, including their name and address. HealthTalker then sent them an information kit plus little business-card-sized brochures to hand out to others. The program encourages HealthTalker members to come back regularly and report how many conversations they've had. But members get no payment. Christine wants people in the program who truly believe in the product, not just those willing to talk about it for some sort of compensation.

In pharma marketing, the objective is to educate patients and make them aware (in a way that's fair and balanced, in compliance with FDA regulations). The patients who hear about Synvisc-One through HealthTalker members arrive at a special Web site where they can request more information, the first step in going to an orthopedist and getting treatment. Christine can track the success of the program through visits and requests for information that come from this site.

Genzyme's HealthTalker pilot generated fifteen hundred conversations in just three months at the end of 2009. The fans in the program are talking to more and more acquaintances, not just friends and family. These are highly qualified leads—people with knee pain who are hard to identify any other way. Based on this level of success, Christine and Genzyme are expanding the program in 2010. There's no more fervent advocate than a person who's gotten relief from suffering.

putting it all together

Taken together, Genzyme, the NHL, and Microsoft can give you a good perspective on the long-term value of fan marketing. Word of mouth is one of the hottest trends in marketing—if you want to learn more, check out Andy Sernovitz's book *Word of Mouth Marketing*[21] or the annual conference of WOMMA, the Word of Mouth Marketing Association.

But let's take a step back. You've now completed the part of empowered that talks about outreach to customers. How does fan marketing fit in?

We've talked about how you need to play defense, using monitoring to see what people are saying and reaching out with service. Because at any moment, a customer you haven't served could start to stomp on your brand very publicly. Or, you could turn that person into a fan.

We've talked about empowering your customers with mobile information rather than letting them find whatever happens into their iPhones, BlackBerry phones, and Androids.

And we've talked about how to go on the offensive, finding your fans, energizing them, and amplifying their impact on other customers and potential customers.

Any organization that wants to enable HEROes to pursue these goals has to change. It's not enough to support these new forms of marketing and customer service. The management needs to change, to give the HEROes more autonomy. The IT department has to change, from running technology to supporting technology projects created by others. And if the company is truly serious about HERO-powered innovation, it needs to put systems in place to help HEROes collaborate with one another.

In the first half of this book, we've told you what to do to reach out to empowered customers. In the second half, we'll describe how organizations full of empowered people can run without spinning out of control. It all starts with the agreement among HEROes, managers, and IT that we call the HERO Compact, as we describe in chapter 7.

the HERO-powered business

7. do-it-yourself technology fuels the HERO Compact

HEROes pick their own technologies. They also make mistakes.

Take Gary Koelling and Steve Bendt, two Best Buy advertising staffers who launched Blue Shirt Nation, an internal social network for the company's "blue shirt" retail sales staff. Here's how we told the story in *Groundswell*:[1]

> Gary started in August 2006 by finding a spare server, stashing it under his desk, and loading it with Drupal, an open-source suite of community-building software . . . The project took off when they showed it to the senior VP of marketing, Barry Judge, who told them that they weren't thinking big enough—and promptly offered them a generous budget to build out the community.

When we reconnected with Gary and Steve in 2009, we were surprised to learn that after a lot of initial success, Blue Shirt Nation was about to shut down. What happened? As it turned out, for Best Buy, Drupal was not the right platform for the long run.

Gary told us, "Drupal gets you 80 percent of the way there, really fast." But as Steve points out, they had to give up on Blue Shirt Nation because the platform needed to reach managers, not just blue shirts, and managers had different needs. "Employees could upload video and pictures. They could create groups . . . But one problem we ran into was the adoption of top management, like general managers [of stores]. They didn't have the time to sit down at a Web portal every day . . . 'How do we work? Well, we work with [Microsoft] Outlook, we work with our phones.' We needed a platform that could plug into those channels."[2]

Since managers were insisting on it, the platform would have to work with BlackBerry phones, text messaging, and corporate email. Best Buy's corporate group, working with IT, rolled out wikis and discussion forums on Microsoft SharePoint that could meet these requirements. Combined with some custom software, the result was very popular. When the time came to shut down Blue Shirt Nation, most of the activity had already migrated to the more robust systems.

You could easily draw the lesson from this that allowing marketing people or other nontechnology staff to provision—that is, acquire and install—their own technology is a mistake. Gary put a server under his desk with Drupal, and it didn't do the job. Isn't that proof that HEROes deploying technology just create problems?

But before you accept that conclusion, look at what Blue Shirt Nation brought to Best Buy. "Before Blue Shirt Nation, there was a lot of mistrust between corporate and the field," Steve says. And as Gary told us, "It led to a big cultural change. Answers used to come from corporate. Now there is more and more focus on retail and store employees as the place where the answers come from, and where people have tools to make a difference."

Out of Blue Shirt Nation came change. It spawned Twelpforce, which empowered staff to help with Twitter support, as you read in chapter 1. Barry Judge learned to embrace ideas not just from his staff, but from customers. And the new system, the better system—the one that managers can use with Outlook and their phones—would never have been created were it not for Blue Shirt Nation. Blue Shirt Nation, a system created by a couple of guys in the advertising department, showed Best Buy what was possible and how to embrace the HEROes in its workforce.

So calling Blue Shirt Nation a technology mistake misses the point. HEROes don't operate at the speed of IT, they move at the speed of the groundswell—and as a result, they *need* to provision their own technology. That's how cultural change starts. And should they experience success, like Blue Shirt Nation did, the IT department needs to help them move from what they've built to a system that the company can run on.

the HERO Compact: IT, managers, and HEROes

The story of Blue Shirt Nation highlights a fundamental challenge for the HERO-powered business. While HEROes are a force for innovation and they serve empowered customers at Internet speed, they also make mistakes, especially when it comes to technology choices. Often those mistakes leave a mess. The IT department and their managers end up cleaning up those messes. This can lead to a desire to lock things down, shut things down, and keep things safe. Unfortunately, those very impulses also crimp HEROes and slow innovation.

What's a company to do?

In examining hundreds of cases of HERO-driven innovations, we've learned a lot about organizational behavior. We've seen companies like Best Buy, the Philadelphia Eagles, and Intuit where the IT groups, managers, and HEROes have come to a détente; where they've worked out ways to support each other and keep the company thriving while keeping systems safe. We've seen many, many more cases where companies lock down systems, say no to HEROes, and make innovation difficult. HEROes at these companies become discouraged or may give up and quit, leaving the companies unable to respond in the face of empowered customers.

In a HERO-powered business, empowered employees are a continuous force for innovation in service of customers. But it takes three groups working together to make this customer-focused innovation possible and safe: IT, managers, and the HEROes themselves (see figure 7-1).

It's not easy for them all to get along. When they do, it's because they each understand what they're uniquely responsible for and how they work together. We call this new way of thinking the HERO Compact (see box).

FIGURE 7-1

The HERO Compact is at the center of the HERO-powered business

HEROes
• Know customer needs
• Use technologies to serve customers
• Operate safely

**HERO
Compact**

Managers
• Make innovation a priority
• Support HEROes
• Work with IT to manage risk

IT
• Support HEROes with technology
• Scale up solutions
• Provide tools to manage risk

the HERO Compact

In a company that supports customer-focused innovation, managers, IT, and HEROes must work together differently.

- IT is responsible for supporting HEROes with technology innovation, giving leaders the tools to manage risk, and scaling up successful solutions.

- Managers are responsible for making customer-focused innovation a priority, establishing the governance structures to support HEROes, and working with IT to manage the business risk of technology.

- HEROes are responsible for knowing what customers need, experimenting with technologies that solve customer problems, and operating within the safety principles established by IT and managers.

In retrospect, you can see that the successful companies and projects we described in the first half of this book adopted this compact. In the rest of the book, we will formalize this: we will show exactly what a company needs to do—in IT, in management, and with its employees—to make HERO-powered innovation successful.

IT's role in the HERO Compact

Let's start with IT departments and their responsibilities for technology. In the past, IT mostly had two jobs. The first was to build and support big technology projects—corporate databases, core business applications like accounting systems, network infrastructure, servers, and PCs for the information workers in companies. The second was to make sure any systems that these workers used were safe and that they kept data secure and functioned properly.

HEROes threaten both of these jobs.

HEROes are do-it-yourselfers. They pick technologies that often aren't sanctioned by corporate IT. Why is this happening?

For one thing, they are exposed *as consumers* to powerful mobile, video, cloud, and social technologies. They see Facebook and ask, "Why can't we do an employee social network?" They make videos of their kids and say, "I could make training videos." They collaborate in their spare time with fellow volunteers on Google Docs and wonder if their company could use them. Because most of these tools are free or cheap and easy to use, many of your information workers are mastering them right now. We call this trend "technology populism."[3] Researchers at Computer Sciences Corporation (CSC) have called it the "consumerization of information technology."[4] But whatever you call it, it means that new technologies are creeping into every workplace. Even if the PCs are locked down, personal mobile devices that browse the Web aren't—so people end up using their own technologies at work all the time.

The second reason that HEROes use do-it yourself technology solutions is that they live with empowered customers. Whether they're in marketing, sales, or customer support, they are typically directly in touch with customers and their problems and desires. It's just too tempting to solve the problems right then and there with technologies that are readily accessible. Whether it's an account manager prospecting on LinkedIn or Gary Koelling putting a server under his desk, technology solutions, created by HEROes, spread throughout the organization.

What should an IT department do? They can't run these projects; they are too small and there are too many of them. They can't outlaw all of them either—that's cutting off a huge source of customer-focused innovation. But for an IT professional, employees using do-it-yourself technology feels like a virus invading the body—it's alien. IT's natural reaction is to say no, or at least whoa. After all, it is the CIO and IT group's responsibility to scale and secure the technology the company runs on and stay on the right side of the law. If they don't have a part in selecting and deploying the tool, they get very nervous.

IT needs to take on a new role, as *a key advisor* to HEROes and their managers, a role we will describe in detail in chapters 12 and 13.

First of all, it's IT's job to help HEROes pick the right technologies. In the Best Buy example at the start of this chapter, IT helped make the transition to the right platform for Best Buy's internal sharing software. In the next chapter, you're going to see how the CIO at PTC, a software company, helped marketing staffers pick the right platform for an online community. More and more, supporting technology innovation as a trusted counselor will become the IT manager's role.

IT also must help manage technology risk. Take iPhones. One IT manager at a global insurance company described it to us this way. "I know I'm going to have to support the iPhone. Everybody is asking for it. Even my CEO wants to know when I'm going to let him use his iPhone. But my problem with iPhone right now [in April 2009] is that I can't yet stand up in front of a judge and explain how it meets our compliance requirements. And that's part of my job." While IT cannot eliminate risk, it is the IT group's role to assess and mitigate risks that come from HERO projects.

IT must also scale up the HERO solutions that work. This is where IT's traditional role intersects HERO initiatives most directly.

Finally, IT must be involved with corporate systems designed to improve employee innovation and collaboration, the systems we will describe in chapters 10 and 11.

IT's pledge in the HERO Compact

- I will focus more on customer-facing opportunities in addition to systems, risks, and operations.

- I will respect requests for new technology support and find ways to say, "Yes, and" rather than automatically saying, "No."

- I will explain the reasons for locking down new technologies and immediately begin looking for ways to unlock them. I will reexamine decisions to lock down new technologies at least once a year.

- I will focus on technology innovation as a core skill so I can counsel HEROes when they come with technology ideas.

- I will question the default assumption that people using do-it-yourself technology are creating risks or wasting time.

- As new HERO projects get off the ground, I will seek ways to help HEROes and their managers scale them up successfully and keep them safe.

- I will focus on training people about risks at least as much as on implementing lock-down technology solutions.

- I will help with the development of corporate systems to promote innovation and collaboration.

In the new world, IT is a driver, protector, and supporter of HERO-powered technology projects. This requires a change in mind-set. We've assembled the elements of this change into a short document called "IT's Pledge in the HERO Compact" (see box).

management's role in the HERO Compact

Just as IT needs to redefine its role, so must managers. For a company to become a HERO-powered business, managers must change their mind-sets as well.

Senior leaders must focus on encouraging innovation. But to prevent chaos, that innovation can't be random; it must align with corporate strategy. In a company that wants more innovation, leadership has to communicate its goals and strategies more effectively or there will be a lot of wasted innovation. To encourage innovation, management needs to support HERO efforts not just with lip service, but with its behavior, by focusing on learning from mistakes rather than on punishing mistakes.

An emblematic example comes from Jeff Bezos at Amazon.com. Jason Kilar, currently CEO of Hulu, used to run Amazon's DVD business. He once ran an experiment in which half the people who looked at DVDs got one price, and half got a lower price. It blew up into a huge embarrassment, with people making accusations that the company was discriminating. As he told *Wired* magazine:[5]

> I emailed Jeff Bezos as soon as I found out. He summoned me to a
> conference room. It was definitely not an enjoyable walk down there.
> I'd been at Amazon for only three years, and I didn't have the luxury of
> a ton of experience to fall back on. But once I got into that room, the
> tone was exactly the opposite of what I expected. All Jeff wanted to
> know was what had happened and what was the best thing we could
> do at that point. The next morning he appeared on the CBS *Early
> Show* and explained everything. It was a defining moment for me.

That's how senior leaders encouraging innovation behave. What about the other managers in these companies?

The manager of a HERO is in a crucial position. Often HEROes don't have all the political skills necessary to take a project from idea through to completion, and they need help from their managers to deal with other affected departments, including IT. HEROes may also lack the perspective to understand whether their idea will actually help customers or not, while managers can often see this more clearly. As a result, managers become key allies as HEROes' innovations go from ideas to actual projects.

Like IT, managers have a role in the HERO Compact. Their responsibilities are focused around tolerance of experiments and ways to support projects appropriately, as we describe in "Management's Pledge in the HERO Compact" (see box).

management's pledge in the HERO compact

- I will articulate and continually communicate the customer goals of the organization and of my department, so that each employee can understand them and pass them along to others.

- I will provide the governance and policy to help HEROes come up with creative solutions that are in line with our goals.

- I will encourage experimentation to solve customer problems where needed.

- I will expect mistakes and failures. I will seek learning from those mistakes and failures, rather than focusing on punishment.

- When HEROes come to me for help, I will seek ways to support their projects by carefully evaluating them and working with other managers to solve the challenges they create.

- I will respect assessments of technology risk in HERO projects and work with IT and others to quantify, mitigate, and ultimately manage that risk.

the HERO's role in the HERO Compact

We've talked a lot about HEROes in this book so far. But HEROes don't work alone; they need to function as part of a corporation. And they need IT's help. In chapter 2, we talked about how Rob Sharpe at Black & Decker needed a video server and IT support to provide the video library that his sales training needed. And Ross Inglis at Thomson Reuters needed serious support and development help from IT to build the independent financial advisor portal. The bigger the project, the more it grows beyond what a HERO can do alone.

It's a two-way street. Even as IT and managers need to respect the HERO's need to experiment with new technologies to solve customer problems, HEROes need to respect IT's and managers' priorities. HEROes can succeed only if they work within the boundaries set up by the company—perhaps near the edges of those boundaries, but not beyond.

What can managers and IT groups expect in the way of appropriate behavior from HEROes? To begin with, HEROes must prove that their projects serve customers. They must work with managers and IT to make sure those projects are safe. They also have a responsibility to other HEROes to spread what they learn, just as Gary Koelling and Steve Bendt spread their knowledge to kick off a whole slew of new projects at Best Buy. The HERO's mind-set complements the mindsets of IT and management, as we describe in "The HERO's Pledge in the HERO Compact" (see box).

do-it-yourself technology in the workplace

The first and most obvious place that HEROes, managers, and IT come into conflict is on corporate PCs and smartphones. What sorts of technologies should employees be able to use in their workplaces? Is it acceptable to use devices, applications, and Web sites that aren't sanctioned by the company?

Let's analyze this from the perspective of the three groups in the HERO Compact.

IT people have a strong incentive to block application downloads, block access to many types of Web sites (including social networks), and stop mobile devices from connecting to corporate systems. People could be downloading viruses. They could create desktop configurations that IT can't support, and that interfere with corporate applications. Their applications use up corporate bandwidth. It's simplest just to ban these activities.

Managers, too, may decide that their workers will be wasting time and productivity on these activities. Why not just stop people from playing around when they should be working?

The problem, from the HERO's point of view, is that many of the best customer-facing ideas require using these online resources and accessing these sites. Would Gary Koelling and Steve Bendt have come up with the idea for Blue Shirt Nation if they hadn't used Facebook? As Irving Wladawsky-Berger, the strategy executive who helped revitalize IBM, puts it, "If you are in an organization where people don't

the HERO's pledge in the HERO Compact

- I will respect the influence of empowered consumers.

- I will explore technologies that can help solve customer problems.

- If my projects entail a significant effort, I will work with my managers and IT to better understand the long-term impact of those projects.

- Where a project creates a risk, I will work with IT and management to understand that risk, assess it, and when possible, mitigate it.

- I will seek ways to take lessons from projects and spread them throughout the organization.

- I will work with other HEROes in innovation and collaboration systems, if the company has those systems.

- When I have access to do-it-yourself technologies, I will use them to advance the business, not for personal or recreational purposes.

participate in the social media discussion both externally and internally, it slows everything down." HEROes need access to these resources. It's awfully hard to develop projects around tools like social networks, video, and mobile devices if you can't even use them at work!

Both sides of this argument have justification. Here's where we come down: companies should block as little as possible, but IT, managers, and employees should work together to manage risk and explore alternatives to find an acceptable solution. That's the HERO Compact. To help support those decisions, let's take a look at just how prevalent unsanctioned access is, and what the consequences of locking down technology would be.

how prevalent is do-it-yourself technology in the workplace?

In the same online survey we used to examine the behavior of people as consumers, we asked people to tell us about their use of technology at work. Of the slightly more than ten thousand people in our survey, 4,364 were information workers—people who work with a computer. This group includes administrative staff, call center workers, and even some shop floor staff and cashiers along with traditional office workers.

More than one in three of the information workers in our survey used some form of do-it-yourself technology for work (see table 7-1). More than 10 percent used smartphones, and of those, the majority had provided the phone themselves. About one in seven information workers were downloading applications to work computers. But the biggest self-provisioned technology is Web sites that employees use that aren't sanctioned by IT. The most popular sites among information workers in the United States, Canada, and the United Kingdom were sites with productivity tools like Google Docs and social networking sites like LinkedIn (see figure 7-2).

TABLE 7-1

Many information workers use do-it-yourself technology

	NUMBER OF EMPLOYEES IN THE ORGANIZATION		
	100 or fewer	**101 to 999**	**1,000 or more**
Self-provision some technology (Web sites, applications, smartphone or mobile plan)	36%	37%	37%
Regularly use unsanctioned login-required sites for work	25%	31%	27%
Download and use applications on work computer	13%	12%	12%
Pay for smartphone used for work	8%	7%	8%
Pay or help pay for mobile plan used for work	9%	9%	9%

Base: U.S. information workers.

Source: Forrester's North American Technographics Empowerment Online Survey, Q4 2009 (US).

FIGURE 7-2

Web sites and services that information workers use

You mentioned that you have used a service on a Web site to help you do your job. What type of service did you use?

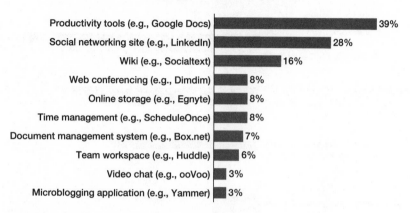

Productivity tools (e.g., Google Docs) — 39%
Social networking site (e.g., LinkedIn) — 28%
Wiki (e.g., Socialtext) — 16%
Web conferencing (e.g., Dimdim) — 8%
Online storage (e.g., Egnyte) — 8%
Time management (e.g., ScheduleOnce) — 8%
Document management system (e.g., Box.net) — 7%
Team workspace (e.g., Huddle) — 6%
Video chat (e.g., ooVoo) — 3%
Microblogging application (e.g., Yammer) — 3%

Base: 947 U.S., Canadian, and U.K. information workers who have used a service found on a Web site to help do their job (multiple responses accepted).
Source: Forrester's Workforce Technographics US, Canada, UK Benchmark Survey, Q3 2009.

Why do workers use do-it-yourself technology? The most common reasons are that they are exposed to it at home, as a consumer, or that they need it and the company doesn't provide it (see figure 7-3). Many feel they have better technology at home than they do at work.

But if you really want to know what's driving this behavior, just listen to the people who are doing it. Here are some of the reasons the people in our survey gave for using do-it-yourself technology in their jobs:

Because it is easier and faster than what is provided at work. And it gives better results.

Getting the job done requires multiple resources and to do my job to the best of my abilities I use all available resources.

The ones they prefer are slower, less organized, and hinder my performance, causing me to take longer to do simple tasks.

I am a physician and there are several sites that augment what is available for me through my employer. Having access to these sites improves my ability to provide for my patients.

FIGURE 7-3

Employees use do-it-yourself technology because it solves problems

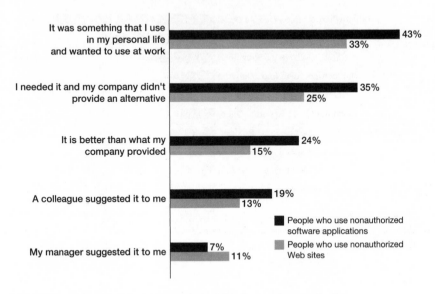

Why are you using nonauthorized software applications, Web sites, or Internet services for work purposes?

- It was something that I use in my personal life and wanted to use at work: 43% / 33%
- I needed it and my company didn't provide an alternative: 35% / 25%
- It is better than what my company provided: 24% / 15%
- A colleague suggested it to me: 19% / 13%
- My manager suggested it to me: 7% / 11%

■ People who use nonauthorized software applications
■ People who use nonauthorized Web sites

Base: U.S. information workers who use nonauthorized Web sites or software applications (multiple responses accepted).

Source: Forrester's North American Technographics Empowerment Online Survey, Q4 2009 (US).

My software needs advance faster than the company's process of testing, setting policies, and distributing software.

I use Google Docs most of all because: 1) the storage is practically unlimited and can be accessed from any computer; 2) it is always up to date with the latest version; and 3) I don't have to worry about a computer crash.

LinkedIn is a great way of keeping track of clients when we are trying to drum up new business.

The software and applications I use are integral for accomplishing my job. The IT geeks are idiots and will not allow anything other than [their] approved programs.

I access my personal e-mail and the Facebook application at work because sometimes my clients contact me through them.

These are people trying to do their jobs better. But in many cases, the company is determined to stop them. In another survey we found that most information workers had sites blocked by their employers: 68 percent in the United States, 69 percent in Canada, and 79 percent in the United Kingdom. For every worker who's trying to do the job better with her own tools, even more are trying to obey the company's rules. Their reasons are much more consistent—you can hear the fear talking:

I can't download anything without an administrative password. Not even updates on authorized software. It's a pain!

At my company, our server has most unauthorized sites blocked and we are not authorized to add new software on our computers. I couldn't do these things even if I wanted to.

I don't want to get in trouble. I have signed many user agreements in which I said I would not.

Because the IT guy in charge of the central computer would have a fit, that's why.

Because you will get FIRED!!!!

assessing the risks and benefits of do-it-yourself technology

According to the HERO Compact, we should carefully analyze a problem like people using unsanctioned devices, applications, and sites in the workplace instead of just rejecting it out of it hand. What are the risks and benefits?

We've already described the risks, which center mostly around security and productivity. But you might be surprised about some of the benefits.

For example, we heard this story from an IT executive in a multinational construction firm in 2010. The company had just implemented a snazzy new telephone and Web conferencing system. Once this rolled out, the IT security group took the opportunity to do something it had been hoping to do for a long time—it blocked people on its corporate networks from using Skype, the Internet telephone software, and thereby hoped to reduce network congestion and improve security. What happened next surprised everybody—a stream of profane calls and emails from some extremely upset employees. Were these people annoyed they couldn't call their friends on vacation in Tahiti? No, as it turned out, the company's customers in Pakistan and Vietnam were completely dependent on Skype for telephone communication, and the company had just cut them off. (In the end the company relented and restored access to Skype.)

IT and management at your company need to create a chart like table 7-2 to decide what sites and behaviors need to be blocked. But you might need to think a little broadly about the benefits, and figure out if there is the equivalent of a free, necessary technology like Skype in use at your own company.

Finally, consider this. Blocking every possible dangerous site is pretty much impossible, especially when people are using mobile phone browsers, not just corporate PCs. You're probably better off keeping an eye on this technology and how people use it, rather than trying to squash it. The more you block, the more you send the message "We don't trust you with new technologies." It's hard to get people to innovate when this is what they're hearing.

putting the HERO Compact into action

As IT, managers, and HEROes begin this journey toward the HERO-powered business, they need a map. That's what we provide in the rest of this book.

Chapters 8 and 9 are focused on management and culture. Managers need to know how ready their companies are for HERO-powered innovation—we provide tools for assessing and changing that in chapter 8. Chapter 9 is about leadership and governance—how to run a HERO-powered business without creating chaos.

Chapters 10 and 11 describe systems for HEROes. We talk about both systems that help drive innovation (in chapter 10) and systems that help HEROes to collaborate (in chapter 11). These management

TABLE 7-2

Benefits and risks of employee access to do-it-yourself technology

Technologies	Risks	Benefits
Mobile (allow workers to access corporate systems on mobile phones)	• If mobile phones are lost corporate systems could be compromised. • Use of mobile phones during work hours could decrease productivity. • Mobile connections need to be tracked in some regulated industries.	• Workers can check sites and information quickly from anywhere. • Access to corporate systems speeds service and increases productivity of mobile workers. • Workers who learn about mobile applications are most likely to have ideas about mobile solutions for customers.
Video (allow workers to create and host videos and access video-sharing sites)	• Use of video-sharing sites could decrease productivity. • Video created by workers could generate legal liabilities. • Video uploads use server space. • Video streaming can generate network congestion.	• Customer-facing staff can view and react to videos created by customers (e.g., "United Breaks Guitars"). • Video improves communication for many "how-to" types of training and sharing. • Workers who learn about uses of video are most likely to have ideas about video solutions to serve customers.
Cloud (allow workers access to sites and Web services on the Internet)	• Cloud services can generate security risks. • Cloud services can generate network congestion. • Cloud services can decrease productivity.	• Workers may identify sites that are valuable sources of information. • Workers may find cheaper resources to solve computing problems using services like Amazon EC2. • Workers who learn about cloud services are most likely to generate cloud service ideas to serve customers.
Social (allow workers access to social networks sites)	• Use of social networks during business hours can decrease productivity. • Workers may share inappropriate or confidential information on social sites. • Workers may use social sites to network to find a new job.	• Workers can use social networks to make connections with customer and partners. • Workers who have access to social technologies are most likely to generate ideas for social applications and sites to serve customers.

tools for the HERO-powered business are often created and run by IT for the benefit of the company. They can make a huge difference, but they often fail; we'll describe how to make them successful.

Chapters 12 and 13 focus specifically on what IT can do in its new roles driving, supporting, and safeguarding HEROes. If you're an IT professional, chapter 12 tells you how and when to say no, and how to set up principles to keep HEROes safe, while chapter 13 tells you how and when to say yes and support HEROes as they innovate.

We bring it all together in chapter 14, which discusses the new mind-set everybody needs in the world of HERO-powered business.

8. is your company ready for HEROes?

Rachel Nislick and Robin Saitz just wanted to find a new way to reach out to customers. It wasn't their intention to transform their company, but that's what ended up happening.

Rachel is an energetic young woman who runs the Web site for PTC, one of the largest providers of CAD (computer-aided design) and PLM (product lifecycle management) software in the world. In late 2007, she conceived the idea of creating an online community for PTC's customers. As we described in chapter 3, communities have significant benefits, including helping customers to get support, opening up an environment to sound out new product features, and surfacing enthusiastic customers who can become valuable company advocates. So Rachel brought her idea to Robin, her boss, who is an ex-engineer, a senior vice president in PTC's marketing department, and a twenty-year veteran of PTC.

Robin was a believer in the power of the groundswell, so she was receptive to Rachel's idea. The idea percolated for a while. By 2009, the two of them had even picked out a vendor to build the community—Jive Software. Nearly everything was in place except for one important element: buy-in. As the project became more visible, executives from all over the company expressed concerns.

For example, Paul Lenfest, the head of customer service, knew much of the company's revenue came from maintenance contracts, and wondered what the community might do to that revenue stream. Steve Horan, who was PTC's CIO at the time, foresaw problems, too. "I am a huge proponent of communities," he said at the time. "But the challenge is they have already chosen the technology."[1] From his experience with PTC projects in other departments, Steve was worried that the marketing team hadn't fully scoped the requirements for IT personnel, support, and funds.

With these organizational dynamics, Rachel and Robin knew they would get nowhere unless the whole organization could come together behind their plan. Here's how they did it.

First, they decided to stop guessing about the customers and ask them. Our company, Forrester Research, helped them field and analyze a survey that reached over seven thousand customers and prospects. Results of the survey: PTC's customers were overwhelmingly ready to embrace a community.[2] I (Josh) presented this information to many of PTC's senior managers at a meeting at the company's Massachusetts headquarters. The executives asked a lot of questions, and the data helped calm some of their concerns. But the plan wasn't out of the woods yet.

PTC's IT and marketing groups collaborated to create detailed community requirements and a deep technical review of the technology platform, Jive. They looked at alternatives that might fit better with PTC's other technology priorities. In the end, Jive won out, but the difference was, the important technical decision makers at PTC had now bought in on that decision, and the company had a more rigorous perspective on what the software would have to do—and how the value would be measured.

This technical review also gave Robin and Rachel time to win over others in the company. Importantly, they won over Jim Heppelmann, the company's president and COO and a highly respected leader with both customers and staffers. As they geared up to launch the community, momentum was clearly building; product managers who had previously been skeptical started to ask when their products could be included, too. The CMO, CIO, and head of customer service all came on board because Robin had done the work to prove the plan was solid and would have a positive impact on PTC's business.

Between Rachel's original idea in 2007 and the community's launch in 2010, the conception of the community hadn't changed all that much. What had changed was PTC itself. In 2007, Rachel was just a woman with a cool idea for customers. In 2010, PTC was a company that knew how to align all of its contending groups behind a couple of HEROes. Both the project and the company were stronger for it.

the two things your company needs to make HEROes effective

The story of what happened at PTC is typical. HEROes don't just get an idea, line up support, and implement it. They can succeed only with the company behind them.

Building a HERO-powered business is hard. Is your company ready for it?

In the previous chapter, we described how IT, managers, and HEROes need to work together to create the HERO-powered business. Empowered workers are not enough; they can succeed only in a culture that encourages them and supports them with resources. At PTC, the resources were there, but the culture—the leadership—needed to come around to support and guide the ideas Rachel and Robin had started with. At other companies, the encouragement and guidance is there but the resources are locked down. Either flaw can stop HEROes from contributing effectively.

So we have identified two key dimensions of readiness—workers feeling empowered and acting resourceful. We created an instrument to measure them. Using our survey of 4,364 information workers in U.S. companies, we analyzed workers by company, by industry, and by job description on these two dimensions:

1. *Do you feel empowered?* We asked workers whether, when it comes to technology at work, they agreed with the statement, "I feel empowered to solve my own problems and challenges at work." Because most people were inclined to respond positively to this statement, we counted someone as feeling empowered only if their response was eight or higher on a ten-point scale.

2. *Do you act resourceful?* As we saw in the previous chapter, allowing employees to use devices, applications, and sites that aren't
sanctioned by the company is a key prerequisite to their ability
to act resourceful. So we measured whether individuals had
downloaded and regularly used at least two unsanctioned applications to their PCs or regularly visited at least two unsanctioned Web sites requiring a login.

These two dimensions give us a unique view into the capabilities
and frustrations of the potential HEROes within companies. Together,
they generate four possible states of mind for an information worker
within your company (see figure 8-1).

- *Disenfranchised Employees* are neither empowered nor resourceful.
  The 34 percent of all information workers in this quadrant don't
  use unsanctioned applications and don't feel empowered to solve
  problems. They just try to do their jobs. While every company
  needs some workers who just follow orders, very little innovation
  is going to come from these ranks.

- *Rogue Employees* act resourceful, but don't feel empowered. This
  quadrant, which includes 14 percent of all information workers,
  includes people who are running unsanctioned applications even
  though their company doesn't support their creative efforts to
  solve problems. Creative energy is better than complacency, but
  these unsupported efforts are less likely to contribute to the company's useful work. If these people are to contribute in a useful
  way, they need support from their company.

- *Locked-Down Employees* feel empowered, but don't act resourceful. This group of information workers is large, at 34 percent.
  People in this quadrant are pulling along with the company to
  solve customer problems, but since their technology is locked
  down by the company, it's unlikely they'll come up with technology solutions that will actually benefit those customers. You can't
  expect people to paint beautiful pictures if their brushes and
  paints are locked away most of the time. To get more out of this
  group, companies need to provide them with technology
  resources so they can act on their creativity.

FIGURE 8-1

The four types of employees in the workforce HERO Index

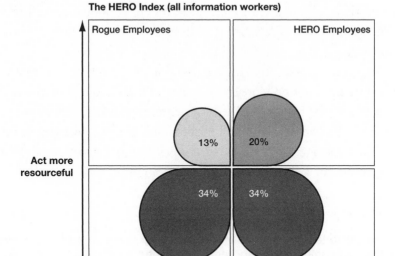

The HERO Index (all information workers)

Rogue Employees | HERO Employees

13% | 20%

Act more resourceful

34% | 34%

Disenfranchised Employees | Locked-Down Employees

Feel more empowered

Base: U.S. information workers.
Source: Forrester's North American Technographics Empowerment Online Survey, Q4 2009 (US).

- *HERO Employees* feel empowered and act resourceful. Here is where technology innovation comes from—the 21 percent of information workers who are using new technologies and know the company wants them to help customers. This is where HEROes come from. All the employee HEROes we've met so far—Rachel Nislick at PTC, Rob Sharpe at Black & Decker, Frank Eliason at Comcast, and Marty Collins at Microsoft—came from this quadrant.

If you want to build a HERO-powered business—if you want customer-focused innovations to arise, get supported, and become part of what makes your company succeed—then your job is to create a culture and a set of resources that pull as many of your best thinkers as possible into the HERO employees quadrant.

where do HEROes come from?

We can use these quadrants to analyze any group of workers. And despite their simplicity, they're highly revealing about where HERO workers come from. We call this analysis the HERO index.

Let's take a look by industry, for example.

The industry with the highest proportion of HERO Employees among its information workers, 37 percent, is technology products and services (see figure 8-2). While this is extreme, it's not unique—workers in business services, media and leisure, and financial services all score well above average. Electronics has not just a high proportion of HERO Employees, but also the highest concentration of Rogue employees of

FIGURE 8-2

The HERO Index shows that more technology products and services workers feel empowered and act resourceful

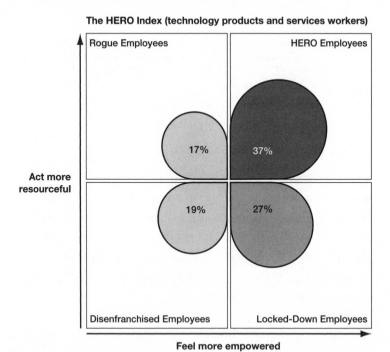

The HERO Index (technology products and services workers)

Base: U.S. information workers in technology products and services companies.

Source: Forrester's North American Technographics Empowerment Online Survey, Q4 2009 (US).

FIGURE 8-3

The HERO Index for government workers

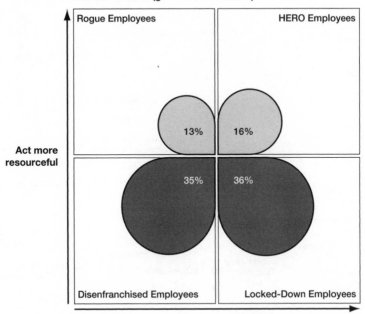

The HERO Index (government workers)

Base: U.S. information workers in government.
Source: Forrester's North American Technographics Empowerment Online Survey, Q4 2009 (US).

any industry. The reasons are clear: technology and electronics are businesses where technology is at the center of innovation, while media and finance are "bit businesses" where companies increasingly compete on their digital delivery (Hulu and E*TRADE are two examples of this). If you're in one of these businesses, you have plenty of HERO employees and your competitors will, too. You must differentiate on how well you lead and manage them.

By contrast, retail had the lowest proportion of HERO employees in our survey, 18 percent. While this is dragged down somewhat by all the people in retail sales, it's a shame, because information workers in retail are exactly the kind of people who would benefit their company by finding new ways to reach out to customers (Best Buy's Twelpforce, which we described in chapter 1, is a great example). Governments, nonprofits,

FIGURE 8-4

Different industries show different levels of empowerment and resourcefulness

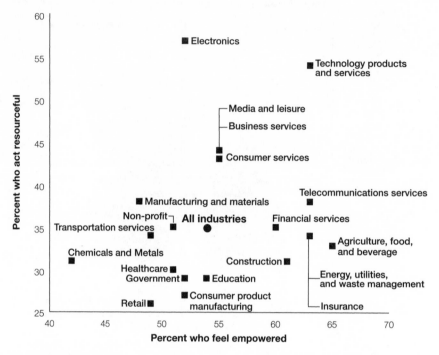

Base: US information workers.

Source: Forrester's North American Technographics Empowerment Online Survey, Q4 2009 (US).

health care, and education also had few employees in the HERO quadrant, which is why HEROes like U.S. State Department staffer Mark Betka from chapter 2 need to be highlighted; most workers in government either don't feel empowered or don't act resourceful (see figure 8-3). In these industries, encouraging HEROes and their innovations can be a significant differentiator against slow-moving competitors.

One other industry is worth examining here: the telecommunications business. Telecom is about average on HERO employees, but 41 percent of its information workers are in the "Locked-Down" segment—employees who feel empowered but don't act resourceful. Innovation in telecom would benefit from managers who encourage more experimentation with technology among their employees, though with safeguards

FIGURE 8-5

Marketing and sales staff are likely to be in the HERO quadrant

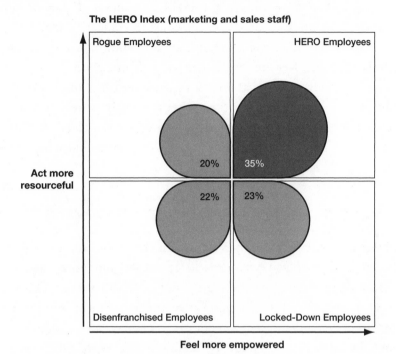

The HERO Index (marketing and sales staff)

Rogue Employees

HERO Employees

20%   35%

Act more resourceful

22%   23%

Disenfranchised Employees

Locked-Down Employees

Feel more empowered

Base: U.S. information workers in marketing and sales, excluding retail sales.
Source: Forrester's North American Technographics Empowerment Online Survey, Q4 2009 (US).

in place to protect against service failures. Given how central new technology services and products will be to telecom, and the rapid rate of evolution of mobile technology, this could make all the difference in a telecom company's future competitiveness.

If you want to compare your industry to the rest of the working world, have a look at the grid comparing all the information workers in our survey by industry (see figure 8-4).

What departments in your organization include the most HEROes? Based on our survey, marketing and nonretail sales have the highest proportion of empowered staff (see figure 8-5). Since it takes an empowered employee to serve an empowered customer, this makes sense. It also means that if your marketing and sales staff *don't* feel empowered, your competitors are probably innovating more than you do. Customer service, on the other hand, is near the bottom, with less than one in five employees in the HERO quadrant. The appropriate visual is a hive of call center workers, stuck in cubicles, unable to contribute meaningfully to the company's ability to innovate in groundswell customer service. (In other words, the opposite of Zappos.)

Unfortunately, even as these service people learn more every day about what's bothering customers, they're mostly unable to use that knowledge to suggest innovations that might solve those customers' problems. What a waste, given the word of mouth that happier customers could create.

two ways to improve your company's culture and readiness

The HERO index is more than an assessment of your company's readiness. It also tells you what to do to create and encourage more HEROes and more innovation and build a HERO-powered business. To get more people into the innovative upper-right quadrant, you can make improvements in two directions: changing your culture to make people feel more empowered, and adding resources (or providing permission to use those resources) to help people act more resourceful.

- *To help more workers feel empowered, improve leadership and management.* HEROes want to create solutions. Companies want people pulling in the same direction, not chaos. This creates tension. The solution is to align your management and culture with HEROes. The PTC case is a great example of what HEROes can do when they're aligned with management—and also of how this process can take a while.

- *To help more workers act resourceful, support them with technology.* HEROes need help. They need access to technology, not locked-down systems. They need tools to help them collaborate, support from technology professionals, guardrails to keep their solutions safe, and systems that spread their success across the organization. For a great example of how this works, take a look at how the IT department at Sunbelt Rentals used iPhones to create sales HEROes.

CASE STUDY

Sunbelt Rentals empowers its workers with mobile decision making

Sunbelt Rentals is filled with employees who feel empowered. They really want to help customers. But it took John Stadick a few tries to figure out the resources they needed.

Sunbelt rents stuff that construction workers use. Its business depends on the sales guys. The company generates over a billion dollars' worth of construction equipment rentals every year, from huge backhoes to handheld drills, and it all comes down to a salesman talking to a construction manager.

A sales guy (it's nearly always a guy) drives his truck up to a construction site. The construction manager says something like, "I'm going to need two jackhammers tomorrow" or "How much for a high-capacity water pump?" Now the sales guy has to figure out if the equipment is available, and what it should cost. Until recently, that meant checking a price sheet printed out on Monday that might be out of date by Thursday. Or he could call somebody at the branch office on a Nextel phone and hope she got back to him in time to close the sale— before the rep from the competing rental company showed up, that is. A lot of the quotes were seat-of-the-pants, based on what somebody got charged last time. The customers were happy and the sales guys were doing their jobs, but things weren't running efficiently.

John Stadick, the vice president of information technology for Sunbelt, knew this was an information problem. He knew what construction was like; he had worked construction sites while in college. And he had the information the sales force needed in a database he'd built. "We knew we had to find a better way of empowering those guys," John said. "What's the status, what's the price? We had to empower the sales guys to find the piece of information themselves."

His problem wasn't a failure to provide resources. He had tried giving them BlackBerry phones with inventory applications on them. The sales guys wouldn't use them. It was "too hard to find what they needed."

How about laptops with wireless data through a mobile phone network? That didn't work, either. The laptops couldn't handle the grit of a construction site, and they fell off the seats and broke a lot.

Was the sales force just resistant to technology? John didn't think that was the problem. They were problem solvers, after all. But like their customers, they needed the right tools for the job.

Finally, Dean Moore, a senior systems engineer working for John, suggested iPhones. This was a promising idea—the phones connected and made information available quickly, with the kind of interface that sales guys could master. So John, Dean, and a developer built an app that could show inventory and pricing. It took about four months to connect the iPhones to John's database. They rolled the phones and apps out to twenty-five local reps, encased in hard-shell "Otter Boxes" that kept the phones safe on job sites. "We built in some tracking tools so we could see what features were being used," John says. "The usage statistics were off the charts." Finally, John had found a solution that would enable the sales force to *act* resourceful. He expanded the pilot and began to measure the results.

Phone calls to the branch offices were down 30 percent. But more importantly, rental rates were up—up 3.5 percent versus a control group that didn't have the iPhones. Because the sales guys no longer quoted from the hip, they were giving accurate rates from the database. Every dollar of that increase went directly to the bottom line. It also helped that they could remind a customer of equipment already rented and, when appropriate, bills that hadn't been paid yet. John rolled out the iPhones to the rest of the sales force.

John figured out how to get his sales force the resources they needed. Now he's got six hundred more resourceful problem solvers coming up with new ideas on how to make his company successful.

how management and IT can support HEROes

In the previous chapter, we talked about the HERO Compact among managers, IT, and HEROes. The tools in this chapter show how to assess your company's readiness to become a HERO-powered business.

Next, we want to provide some practical advice on what managers and IT can do to make this new way of doing business a reality.

Leading HEROes is hard. While you have to give up central control of technology, you must also lead your HEROes so they end up contributing to your business. We tackle this essential contradiction in the next chapter.

9. leading and managing HEROes

Here's what we learned from Scott Cook, the founder of Intuit: fail as frequently as possible. But learn from it.

Intuit is an incredible company in a boring category. Revenues at Intuit went up every year between 2005 and 2009, recession or not. And this is a company that makes solutions for accounting and taxes, chores that most individuals and small businesses think about as little as possible. Even though the consumer software business has been in the dumper for years, with prices dropping and competition commoditizing the products that companies and people *do* buy, Intuit is thriving. The reason: a culture that encourages, nurtures, and supports HEROes.

This business of leading and managing HEROes is tricky. Innovators create disruption. Their ideas can be uncomfortable and threaten others. A lot of them will fail. So a HERO-powered business has to do three things. One, it has to encourage that innovation through leadership, as part of a strategy that everyone at the company understands. Two, HEROes need to be able to test these innovations rapidly, kill what's not working, and scale up the rest. And three, the company needs to encourage HEROes to collaborate across organizational boundaries, because the best ideas almost always cross those boundaries.

When it comes to leading, Intuit's management is holding up its end of the HERO Compact. According to Scott Cook, "Our job is to solve the most important problems in our customers' lives. Our guiding rationale, our mission and belief, is to change people's lives profoundly." This statement doesn't talk about tax or accounting products (Intuit has them) or about software (Intuit sells it)—it talks about people. Those people are generally individuals, families, or small businesses like hair salons and consulting groups. This statement also doesn't talk about business models. This means that if somebody at Intuit comes up with a service rather than a product, or a cloud-based system that delivers value through the Web, those ideas will get a fair shake.

We talked about some of Intuit's innovations that came from this attitude in chapter 4. These days, many of them are connected with tapping empowered customers for help with support or marketing. For example, TurboTax's help feature now calls up an online community, rather than static help content; you'll see what others are saying about, say, depreciation. This has both decreased support costs and increased customer satisfaction. The small-business marketing group has innovated with its hyperlocal "Love a Local Business" feature,[1] which encourages customers to point out other businesses in their local community that are delivering great service. Intuit has volunteer "Insider" panels of tens of thousands that provide feedback on several of its products. It's clear, as you review the way the company runs, that innovative ideas for serving empowered customers are the way Intuit does business, and the innovation can come from anywhere in the company.

What's the result of all this innovation? Many successes, and a lot of failures, too. Scott Cook loves failures, so long as they're useful failures. "We have a high tolerance for experiments," he explains. "One of the biggest things I have learned in business is the importance of fast, cheap experiments and high velocity. If you want systemic innovation, make it fast and cheap for people to try things, and painless to fail. Experiments: most of them will fail." What's the penalty for failing at Intuit? "The consequence is learning and admiration for the learning."

This is not lip service. Intuit changes something on its TurboTax Web site every week, then analyzes the results. As Scott puts it, "This allowed lots of different people in marketing to try things which were not restricted by the orifice of management." Its QuickBooks product for small-business accounting now gets updates every month; the company reviews the usage and makes changes accordingly. Change, experimentation, and improvement are baked into the culture.

You might think all this experimentation would create chaos. And it does sometimes. But Intuit manages the chaos with systems that help the most promising innovations to bubble up. "Brainstorm" is an internal system at Intuit where any employee can enter an idea; other workers can not only vote, but comment and make their own suggestions. Exciting ideas get collaborators and move quickly through the process.

Take its new ViewMyPaycheck service. If you work for a big company, your paycheck probably goes through ADP or Paychex, and you can see your pay stubs online. Some HERO in the Tucson office proposed a similar system for Intuit's small-business payroll service.

Since small businesses generate only a few paychecks each month, this might seem like a minor idea.

Except that in aggregate, 14 million people get their paychecks every month from Intuit's payroll service. By creating a Web site they can all go to, Intuit created a channel to 14 million consumers. Marketers in the other consumer divisions, like TurboTax and Quicken, were delighted.

Intuit has figured it out. Fail frequently. And generate your ideas in a place where all the departments can see them.

the tension between chaos and management

Did it make you uncomfortable to read about all the experiments and failures at Intuit? It should. It's not so easy to create a culture that tolerates experimentation this way. Companies are set up so that people are responsible for departments, for goals, for generating revenue, keeping costs under control, and taking credit. An atmosphere of wild experimentation seems counterproductive. What if it damages your brand? What if it cannibalizes a revenue stream? What if it wastes money, upsets the sales commissions, gives competitors an opening? It's a whole lot easier to keep doing things the way you've always done them.

Clayton Christensen describes this challenge in his book *The Innovator's Dilemma*.[2] As he points out, the problem is that somebody, probably at a start-up, is already pioneering the innovations you find so threatening. They are reducing costs, reaching out to empowered customers, or just coming up with new ideas. The market, as a whole, tolerates a lot of failures punctuated by the occasional breakthrough success. Most companies don't, so they get out-innovated.

HERO-powered businesses will find these new solutions. If you compete with them, they will leave you behind. You have to find a way to *manage* the chaos of HEROes innovating all around your company. That's what this chapter is about. We understand how uncomfortable this is, so we'll show you how to build systems to boost innovations that support, rather than torpedo, corporate strategy.

There are two sides to getting HEROes to deliver actual results for your company. First you'll have to lead them. Then you'll have to manage them.

leadership that generates HEROes and serves strategic goals

Look at how Scott Cook and Intuit have created an innovative environment. But leadership that tolerates experiments and innovation does not mean abandoning corporate strategy. At Intuit, that strategy remains around delivering financial solutions to small businesses and consumers. Innovations intended to serve huge companies, give away value for free, or take Intuit into the entertainment business wouldn't fit that strategy. HEROes with ideas like these probably wouldn't find support for their innovations within Intuit, regardless of how inexpensive or exciting their ideas were.

At Intuit, HEROes are serving current strategy. What about when you're changing strategy? Then you need HEROes and their innovations even more.

Take the example of Vail Resorts, a company that operates multiple properties, including five major ski resorts. The company used to place ads in long-lead publications like *Ski* magazine and hope that people seeing those ads in August or September might book a December or January ski vacation. But those ads had become less and less effective because skiers were shifting increasingly to booking vacations just a few weeks or days in advance. The company needed the flexibility to create pitches based on current conditions—snowfalls, competitors' promotions, local events. Long-lead magazines can't do that.

As a result, Vail Resorts' CEO Rob Katz decided to change his marketing completely.[3] The advertising focus shifted to short-lead media, like newspapers and online sites. The other focus was the social technologies of the groundswell, where many of the ski customers were getting their information. "We needed to be a leader in [the social] space, rather than battle the trend of where our customers are going," he says.

Rob hired Mike Slone, a veteran of the interactive development house Razorfish, to head up social engagement in the new marketing strategy. Mike manages a team of five in Vail Resorts' corporate headquarters who respond to tweets, blogs, and other social inquiries. And Mike's team also works to involve other staff, including the heads of online marketing at each of the company's five mountain resorts and other staff who create content for social sharing. "We see social becoming part of everyone's job here," says Mike. Vail Resorts is amplifying its fan activity, just like Microsoft and the NHL in chapter 6.

Crucial in examples like Vail Resorts and Intuit are the signals from the top. In the case of Vail, CEO Rob Katz demonstrates that he really supports all the social activity by tweeting himself, as @rickysridge. When a customer named Bob Lefsetz tweeted about a problem signing up for a meal pass, Rob made sure he got what he was looking for. (This turned out to be very smart, since Bob Lefsetz was a guy with almost thirteen thousand Twitter followers and a popular blog in the music industry; his followers and blog readers got to read about how great Vail is[4]—instead of another "United Breaks Guitars"–style rant.)

Before we leave the topic of leadership, there's one more leader we'd like to cite: Barry Judge, the CMO of Best Buy. As you saw in chapter 1, Best Buy encourages customer-facing employees to be HEROes. In addition to Twelpforce, Best Buy continues to innovate in surprising ways. Barry posts commercials on his blog before they go on TV—and has in some cases changed or pulled them based on blog comments. The company opened up the API (application programming interface) for its Web site, enabling other sites to take feeds of product specs and prices and make new interfaces for them—and also to feed traffic to the Best Buy site. These are HERO-driven innovations that the company encouraged.

But what's most fascinating is Barry's attitude. When it comes to new ideas, "we're almost always in a half-baked mode," he says. "Half-baked ideas allow people [both internally and externally] to give you feedback." Barry recognizes that marketers must always be learning. As he puts it, "If you are not curious, you won't last long in marketing. I used to be, perceptually, the smartest guy in the room. It takes some time to realize that makes you the dumbest thing in the room. You have to have some personal failures to help see that."

What do Scott Cook, Rob Katz, and Barry Judge have in common? They live up to their part of the HERO Compact. They articulate a clear strategy so people know what the goal is. They encourage people to do lots of experiments, failures, and half-baked stuff to surface the best ideas. They recognize that what works often comes from some unexpected direction, so they're open to all sorts of innovation. And by rewarding that innovation, they encourage more of it.

Fine, we hear you saying. Innovation is great. It's just that this level of chaos isn't tolerable at my company. But in fact, these companies aren't chaotic—they're encouraging innovation in a systematic, efficient way. That's where governance comes in—there has to be a way to channel all this activity productively. That's what Manish Mehta learned at Dell.

CASE STUDY

Dell governs the chaos with a council

Dell has embraced social technologies more than any other company in the world, with over a hundred different programs scattered around the world. Manish Mehta, Dell's vice president of social media and community, has the job of making sense of this cacophony. Manish showed us the results on a map, with colored dots representing social initiatives in the United States, Latin America, Europe, China, India, and worldwide. There is a dot for Dell's use of Twitter to drive $7 million of computer sales in the United States. There's the Brazilian Facebook community. Add several different flavors of IdeaStorm, Dell's program to get customers suggesting and voting on new product ideas. Plus, there are internal projects, like the employee wiki they use in India. Manish's world map looks like it has the chicken pox.

Dell got to this spot with leadership from the company founder. In 2006, even before he had returned to the CEO role, Michael Dell had encouraged the use of social applications to reconnect the company with its customers. It worked. But now it was time to take all this activity and make it work in a concerted way.

Manish's job is to assemble a profitable, measurable global social media and community strategy from the one hundred colored dots. This is a job that takes not heavy-handed management, but persuasion. His efforts need to cut across the boundaries of Dell's geographies and departments, to cut through the politics and share the best practices.

Manish's first move was to charter a new Social Media and Community Governance Council, with the intention of bringing coherence to social technology efforts and maximizing benefits across the company. This diverse group of a dozen managers includes representatives from each business unit, even those far from consumer markets, and each major region as well as from IT, legal, employee communications, HR, and marketing. Each is a direct report to the head of one of Dell's departments or units. Manish leads the council in weekly ninety-minute meetings and sets its agenda. (While Manish reports to the CMO, this is by far the least important element of his councils—since councils are cross-functional, the people who manage them can be in IT, marketing, product management, PR, HR, or many other parts of the organization, depending on where the center of activity is.)

First and foremost, the council governs the social technology investments and policies for customers and for employees. This means constructing and ratifying the social strategy, the employee appropriate-use policies, the funding model, and the business metrics. It means turning a hundred separate initiatives into a strategy for harnessing empowered customers and employees to Dell's advantage. The group talks about metrics, vendors, challenges, and successes in an attempt to standardize, scale up, and measure the effectiveness of similar efforts in different departments.

Second, this group taps into the employee groundswell to find and share best practices from across the organization. It could be using

Twitter in the United Kingdom to sell computers at the Dell outlet, a practice pioneered by the U.S. regional team. Or it could be sharing an internal use of social media.

To maximize the opportunity of finding and sharing best practices, Manish has implemented a "hub-and-spoke" model for his council. Each of his council members has her own subcouncil made up of key members of her organization. For example, the consumer business subcouncil has representatives from sales, marketing, product development, and customer service. In this way, the council extends its reach and multiplies the chances that it will hear about a good idea and be able to help shape and spread it across the company.

HERO projects start small. Then they get bigger. Then they spread and become strategic. In a company the size of Dell, it makes sense to manage them in cross-functional councils. The objective is not to squash the ideas. The objective is to generate more of them, harness them in a more organized way, and turn them from small successes into powerful drivers of strategy.

why cross-organizational councils make sense

Companies as diverse as Kodak, Cisco, Intel, and Procter & Gamble also use cross-organizational councils to set strategy, define policy, and determine funding to empower employee HEROes.

Notice what these councils are *not*. They are not in charge of all the social applications in the company. They are not responsible for innovation. They are not intended to hem in, shut down, manage, or combine HERO efforts. HERO projects spring up from everywhere because only the individuals most closely in touch with empowered customers and problems can see what's needed and act quickly to meet those needs.

And councils are not just for social technology efforts. The principle of cross-organizational councils is also the right way to tackle the business opportunities presented by mobile, video, or cloud computing applications. Any company big enough to have several applications of this type can benefit from coordinating them, sharing resources, and sharing best practices.

All these technologies spring from workers' personal experience as technology consumers. Everyone feels they can master them. Often, having gotten started, they find themselves a little daunted with technical, organizational, or content creation issues. This is where councils can help.

As part of the HERO Compact, managers should resist the urge to combine similar initiatives under one roof. HERO projects like internal employee social networks and customer social networks share common challenges, but need to be run by very different groups. Training video isn't the same as marketing video. A company like Procter & Gamble might have ten different mobile applications, including some for marketing, some for customer service, and some for supermarket managers. Rather than force-fit these applications into some central organization that will become a bottleneck, it's far better to give HEROes (and their bosses) the opportunity to share with others across the organization. (It also makes sense to give them online tools for sharing, as we'll describe in the next chapter.)

So, if you're going to start a council for HEROes or managers involved in similar projects, how should you go about it? We recommend five principles.

1. *Councils have CEO or executive-level support.* Without this executive charter, the council will have no mandate to implement its decisions. It becomes simply a working group that makes recommendations. Executive sponsorship is another way for leaders like Michael Dell or Scott Cook to show they're supporting a HERO-powered business.

2. *Councils should include a representative from every relevant group.* It's not a groundswell council if it's staffed by people from a single business group, or all reporting to the CMO, or all part of IT. Councils have to include a representative from every group that might care—or block—the decisions, including IT. At Intel, for example, the chief information security officer, Malcolm Harkins, chairs a council that reviews HERO initiatives. The council includes IT, legal, HR, corporate communications, and the relevant business groups.

3. *Councils are staffed with empowered employees.* Councils don't need to be yet another meeting on a senior executive's weekly calendar. But the members must be able to get things done. It's often the pragmatic informal leaders who make the best council members, because they are influential enough in their groups to get things done, but have the time to take on this extracurricular activity.

4. *Councils have a regular meeting cadence.* Councils aren't casual things. At Dell, the Social Governance and Strategy Council meets for ninety minutes every week. At Cisco, the Collaboration Council meets for ninety minutes every two weeks. In Manish's words, "If you meet quarterly, you will fail. If you meet monthly, you will fail. I believe you need to meet weekly, at least in the beginning."

5. *Council agendas span internal and external initiatives.* HERO projects for employees, for customers, and for partners are often similar. At one insurance company, we saw parallel projects for insurance agents, employees, and customers—all benefited from the insights of the others. At Kodak, Bruce Jones, the global manager of security, compliance, and risk management, helped drive a cross-departmental effort to create a comprehensive social media policy that covers expectations and guidelines for social media inside and outside the company.

the importance of systems

This chapter and chapter 8 describe what senior managers need to know to manage the chaos of a HERO-powered business. We've described the metrics and management systems, such as councils, that take HERO-led innovation and turn it into a scalable, companywide, collaborative activity.

But management systems aren't the only systems at work here. Innovation and collaboration systems, based on software but rooted in culture, can make all the difference in uniting and supporting the HEROes in your organization. That's the topic of chapter 10.

10. helping HEROes innovate

Jon Bidwell is the chief innovation officer of the Chubb Group of Insurance Companies, a 128-year-old, multinational, $11 billion company with ten thousand employees.

Read that sentence again. Imagine for a moment you were in charge of facilitating innovation for a huge, old insurance company. How would you generate innovation? Is it even a good idea for an insurance company to innovate?

According to Jon, it's essential. "Most companies that die in this business, die because they become irrelevant, competing on price," he explains. "We want to have the best stuff out there." So Jon helped Chubb to launch an open innovation challenge.

Open innovation is a philosophy that says that the most productive innovation comes from opening up a company to ideas from anywhere, not just from R&D. Among the tenets of open innovation is that innovators are often hatching ideas out in the trenches, where they see the problems customers have. In other words, the job of innovation is to empower those highly resourceful operatives. HEROes again.

Chubb structured its innovation challenge very carefully, to give it the highest likelihood of generating ideas that would move the business.

First, the company selected a limited time period of thirty days and ran, basically, a contest. Using email and the home page on the Chubb intranet, which gets an awful lot of traffic, the company drove employees to a page where they saw messages from Dino Robusto, Chubb's chief administrative officer, and from Jim Cash, a board member and former professor at the Harvard Business School.

Second, Chubb used a software package called Idea Central from Imaginatik, specially designed to present and capture ideas. If you've ever seen idea-generation sites like MyStarbucksIdea or news-ranking sites like Digg, the concept is similar: anyone can create an idea, and others can rate it or comment on it. The rating and commenting is crucial, because for every person who submits an idea there are probably a hundred who have useful opinions on those ideas, even if they don't have the nerve to submit their own. This stirs the pot and gets more people involved, even as it helps the most promising ideas rise to the top.

Third, and just as crucially, Jon involved twenty-four mid- to high-level executives in facilitating the process. They used an Idea Central feature that allowed them to forward ideas to various kinds of experts within the company, with suggestions that those experts comment (as in "Is this legal?" or "Have we tried this before?" or "Can our underwriting systems handle this?").

The process generated 608 ideas. Of these, twenty-four were both ranked highly by their peers and rated as feasible by the company experts. The twenty-four potential HEROes presented their ideas to a group of executives for fifteen minutes each; the group reviewed them all and chose four for further development. Those four teams put together full plans for review by an internal venture capital team.

Of the three ideas that came out of Chubb's first innovation event, one was from Frank Goudsmit, an underwriter in Chubb's life sciences division with twenty-one years' experience. Frank wanted to solve a big challenge faced by the company's biotech and medical device clients. Life sciences clients who run clinical trials of drugs or medical devices in multiple geographies need approval from local institutional ethics boards in each country. The local ethics boards require proof of insurance in the local language and in compliance with local regulations. When time gets tight, the life sciences companies may not allow enough time for insurers to prepare the necessary paperwork, potentially resulting in inaccurate or missing paperwork, delays in running trials, and lost profits.

Frank's idea was to create Web forms and software to automate the process of securing the insurance binder. Instead of human-driven cut-and-paste jobs with Microsoft Word—a process that often ran afoul of time zones as well as deadlines—Chubb would build a system that could generate the insurance binder on the fly.

Once the project was funded, Frank worked on it with Chubb's IT group. While the budget was around a million dollars, the results promised to make Chubb an indispensable international partner for huge multinational life sciences companies, well worth the cost of the investment.

Frank's impression of Chubb is instructive, since it reveals that this sort of change reinforces that innovation is part of the company culture. "I think Chubb has always been a company that recognizes people have good ideas and wants to promote the concept of advancing ideas," he says. "Every organization says it wants to be innovative. But when you see that level of commitment from John Finnegan, our CEO, and all the ideas readily available to anyone to vote or comment on, that proves it."

innovation is about speed, collaboration, and systems

Every worker has ideas. Some of them grow up to be innovations, products, methods, or businesses. Others just stay ideas. How often have you seen an idea and said, "I already thought of that!" How often have you seen a competitor develop an idea that you or your colleagues came up with?

The problem in a HERO-powered business isn't coming up with ideas. The problem is figuring out which of those ideas should be nurtured and which should not. Can you be *systematic* with idea development? As we look at companies that embrace HERO-driven innovation, we've identified three elements that companies need to turn the best ideas from a notion into a project.

1. *Speed.* HERO-driven innovations need to move forward; otherwise their creators, unable to make progress, give up and go back to doing their regular jobs. A company that doesn't act

on innovations trains its staff that innovating is a worthless and unrewarding activity, and shouldn't be surprised when the flow of ideas stops. What Chubb did—setting a time limit and making idea development into an event—is one way to inject speed into the process. Other companies (like Deloitte Australia, which we'll describe later in this chapter, and Intuit) have a process of continuous innovation, but ideas still get quick responses. Fast is better than slow. For a HERO, even rejection is a stimulus to improve an idea or come up with a new one; better a fast "no" than an indeterminate "we'll get back to you."

2. *Feedback from across the organization.* The best ideas cross organizational silos. HEROes typically don't live high enough in the organization to conceive of the challenges, opportunity, and little twists that can take an innovation and make it practical in a corporate environment. Chubb used Idea Central's feature to forward ideas to experts and others within the company. The true value of Intuit's ViewMyPaycheck idea, as described in the previous chapter, wasn't visible until people in Web advertising realized the value of the traffic it would create.

3. *Software that supports innovation.* Imaginatik is one of eleven different software systems that companies use to manage innovation.[1] Innovation management software typically includes tools for moving ideas through various stages of development, ways to track and reward ideas financially, and guided innovation or brainstorming features. Tools like InnovationSpigit allow the best ideas to float to the top, based on voting from other participants. Regardless of their particular format, the best tools enable people across departments to see, sort, and contribute to the ideas that HEROes come up with. But no matter what software you use, make sure it fits in with your company's internal systems; as Matthew Brown, Forrester's expert on innovation management software, recommends, "Examine your enterprise collaboration environment and assess whether innovation software will complement or overlap with existing tools like discussion forums, community workspaces, and social networking tool sets."

While events are great for surfacing ideas, many companies need ways to keep innovation going continuously—a discipline that happens only when people connecting with others around ideas becomes part of the culture. That's what happened at the Australian operation of the global consulting and accounting firm Deloitte.

CASE STUDY

Deloitte Australia Yammers its way to new ideas

Pete Williams is not your typical accountant. He started his career with fourteen years as a chartered accountant and then followed that up with sixteen years in Web development. Now he's the CEO of Deloitte Digital in Australia, the online business of Deloitte Australia.

Deloitte Australia includes Web development and management consulting businesses, not just accounting. Deloitte Australia's forty-five hundred people must cover a continent with widely spread population centers and companies with widely varying needs; as a result, its specialists have diverse skills, from Flash programming to online accounting, and are located all over the country. It has to somehow be big and small at the same time.

With these demands, Deloitte Australia needs—and has—a culture where people are accustomed to helping each other innovate. Pete Williams says there's a phrase that comes up all the time in conversations at the company: "Can I borrow your brain for a minute?" As in "Can I borrow your brain to learn about changes in financial regulations?" or "Can I borrow your brain to help me understand Web analytics?" When you work at Deloitte, you know that people will need to borrow your brain from time to time, and that next week you might need to borrow theirs.

The culture of sharing was present, but the technology for sharing wasn't. Pete changed that.[2]

Pete knew that in a large organization, email is too clogged up and not fast enough for the sharing he needed. A static intranet site can hold known and settled documents, but not the contents of all the brains at Deloitte Australia. So when it came time to figure out how

Deloitte could take innovation to the next level, Pete turned to the simplest, lightest-weight, fastest thing he could find: Yammer.

Yammer is basically Twitter for enterprises. You sign up and start sending out short updates, but only people within your company can sign up to see those updates. As with Twitter, many of those short messages include links to other sites—news items, blog posts, or content on the company intranet. It's free to start up, but if it becomes a serious enterprise tool, you'll likely want the paid professional version. People sign up to follow individuals or groups with whom they share an affinity, or sample the whole company's stream (which is a bit like drinking from a fire hose, with thousands of participants). It's perfect for the "Can I borrow your brain?" culture of Deloitte Australia.

People need a spark to get them to pick up a tool like this. For Deloitte, that spark came from a campaign to generate a tagline for the company. Pete sent out an email asking for tagline ideas, with discussion to follow on Yammer. Adoption of Yammer within the company exploded. The original sixty people who had been testing Yammer grew to hundreds as over fifteen hundred tagline suggestions got posted over a twenty-four-hour period.[3]

Yammer works because it's not just an undifferentiated feed. By subscribing to people you work closely with or to groups, you can make sure you stay connected with what's important in your job. At Deloitte Australia, there are groups for people working on online accounting, groups that keep accountants up to date on the latest changes in accounting rules, and groups that help frequent travelers with tips on how to survive on the road. In eight months, one hundred forty different groups have sprung up.

Yammer supercharges innovation by connecting people who can help. For example, one staffer at Deloitte Australia identified a need to create a benchmarking tool for clients to measure occupational health and safety. "That idea came in and, by the time I got to look through the comments on it, the people who can build it had already hooked up with the people whose idea it was," Pete says. With Yammer greasing the connections, Deloitte was able to get the product ready and into the market in six weeks.

Yammer has now reached over half of Deloitte's Australian operation, and it has met Pete's goals. "Since we incorporated Yammer, the number of ideas has gone through the roof," Pete says. Worried about productivity drain from people yammering on all day long? Pete explains that since it does not require in-the-moment responses like a phone call or an instant message session, Yammer can fit easily into empty moments in the day, as email does; when waiting around for an elevator, for example, people can respond on their mobile devices. Reading and responding to posts takes just a few minutes a day. The flexibility that comes from starting a new group for any problem within or across departments more than makes up for the time spent.

Pete Williams says, "In large organizations, you need to break down silos, create better community, and speed up sharing and collaborating." With Yammer, he's found a way to do that for Deloitte Australia.

big innovations and sustaining innovations

Companies are fond of differentiating between big innovations—hundred-million-dollar ideas—and sustaining innovations—the little fixes and tweaks that HEROes come up with. But in fact, it's often the little HERO innovations that turn into the big ideas over time. Deloitte Australia's Yammer experience and Chubb's innovation contests may have spun off new products and processes, but they also generated hundreds of little innovations as well. While these may not get big funding, they can still move the company forward, and more importantly, they change the culture to be more innovation focused.

Cisco may be the world's best company for fostering innovation. Guido Jouret, a chief technology officer there, makes it his job to find and nurture businesses with billion-dollar potential—businesses that can make an impact on a company as huge and fast-moving as Cisco. But interestingly, Cisco bubbles up ideas from HEROes at the bottom, just like Chubb and Deloitte Australia. Cisco runs software internally called iZone that enables people to suggest ideas and comment on ideas from others. Guido's team pores over the ideas, looking to see which ideas are worthy of investing more effort.

We learned a couple of things from Guido that every company should know. First, he says that "there is a 98 percent attrition rate from ideas to investment." Guido ends up sorting through four hundred to five hundred ideas every year to find just a few whoppers. Cisco's collaborative, innovation-focused culture makes this possible—it's a company of engineers. But without a mechanism to surface and vet hundreds of ideas, there would be no way to find the huge ones. Luckily for Cisco, many of the ideas that aren't big enough for Guido to invest in still get funded at departmental levels. The exhaust from Cisco's HERO-powered culture supports sustaining improvements in all the company's products.

Second, as Guido says, "If you ask employees, you can't expect a fully formed business plan to leap off the page." Guido has a team of ten people helping to develop these ideas to the point where they can be seriously evaluated. Your company probably doesn't need a team of ten. But if you don't dedicate some resources, you'll never know if one of those ideas is *the* big idea that could change your company. Systems and managers who regularly participate in evaluating and supporting innovation are what makes the difference between a culture that is just innovative and one that creates innovations that can power their business.

innovation, collaboration, and the HERO Compact

Innovation systems are another great example of the HERO Compact. Management needs to supply the culture, the incentives, and the direction to potential HEROes. The IT group is typically responsible for deploying the software system, like Imaginatik or Yammer in the examples we've shown here. The HEROes need to put their ideas through the system to benefit from the counsel of others across the organization. Unless all three approach innovation with a new mindset, the results will be disappointing.

But once the ideas have begun, there's another need—a need to collaborate. The most interesting and most valuable HERO projects typically involve cross-functional teams from across the organization. Traditional tools like email aren't sufficient for the intensity of collaboration that's required.

In fact, the best collaboration tools are those that mimic what's going on outside the enterprise, in the consumer groundswell. Internal sharing tools are social networks whose members are employees, not consumers. Those collaboration tools are the topic of the next chapter.

11. helping HEROes collaborate

BBVA is exactly the kind of company that needs collaboration most.

Starting as Banco de Bilbao in 1857, BBVA grew into a global financial powerhouse, the second-largest bank based in Spain, with over one hundred ten thousand employees in thirty countries and 47 million customers. Global financial companies aren't known for being nimble; they're known for the internal communication challenges they face.

But BBVA has made collaboration and innovation priorities. When I (Josh) visited the company in 2008 and 2009, I spoke to large and engaged groups of executives in a modern technology center, housed within a renovated old building called the Centro de Innovación, or Innovation Center. The "new within the old" model that describes this building is also a fitting symbol for BBVA and its department of innovation and development. Fernando Summers is head of BBVA's innovation and knowledge management group, a department that must not only come up with innovations, but also stimulate innovation and collaboration among the bank's diverse worldwide staff.

At the center of this initiative is BBVA's Blogsfera, an internal blogosphere visible only to employees, which has grown to five hundred blogs and fifty posts a week in the last two years. There are personal blogs, shared departmental blogs, and blogs convened just for projects; any employee can create or comment on any blog. The purpose is pure and simple information sharing. When BBVA's human resources department became worried about potential abuse in the blogging area, Fernando came up with a simple solution—no one could contribute anonymously; all participants had to log in with their BBVA email. In two years there have been zero abuse problems, because people who blog and comment under their own names in a company forum are unlikely to behave irresponsibly.

The BBVA blogosphere was an attempt to expand beyond the forums and static information tools that BBVA had already implemented—to create something at the same time more personal, more dynamic, and less formal. To get an idea what happens in BBVA's Blogsfera, let's look at an internal blog by Carmen Benito, a thirty-year veteran employee in the bank's risk department. Fernando says that within the bank, the risk department is perceived as "a dark department, on the back side" of the loan activity in the bank. To retail bankers and others writing loans, the risk department's thumbs-up or thumbs-down decisions on loans and investments are sometimes mysterious. In this environment, especially amid the dangerous economics of 2009, Carmen wanted to communicate how the bank sees risk, so she started a blog called Pasión por el Riesgo (Passion for Risk).

True to its name, Carmen's blog took an innovative approach to describing risk, including the risks that come from the bank's portfolio of equity and loan investments—a hot topic given the pressure diversified banks are under. Tapping into Spaniards' appreciation for great food, she used this "recipe" to communicate how the company evaluates and manages risks (the original was in Spanish, of course, and we've included just enough in this excerpt to give you an idea of the style):

Ingredients for a Consolidated [Risk] Group
- Several templates (which are Excel spreadsheets into which information is dumped)
- A ton of stocks (better if local, to give a special touch to the dish)
- Segments (those of different backgrounds to serve Spain, Portugal, USA, Mexico, and South America, where we know there are different varieties)

. . .

Difficulty: High. **Cooking time:** 10 days. **Preparation:** Put the local balances in the Template section, the assets and . . . risk, particularly
credit. Local stocks come, in most cases, from Financial Management which will await the best time of month to collect them at their
true point of maturity . . .

Presentation: Templates of different countries are sent to the Department of Global Risk Management, where they are integrated to ensure
that the dish incorporates the entire capital balance at risk . . .

Tasting: . . . This is a very energetic plate so it is recommended not
to take it more than once a month. Additionally, once a year, coincid-
ing with the feast of the annual report of the Group BBVA, it is cus-
tomary to make a preparation with a special touch, which invites all
shareholders and investors of the Group to share in the tasting.

In posts like this, thirty years of experience unspooled in a very human
display of blogging, and the rest of the bank became smarter about a key
topic for any innovation the bank comes up with.

The BBVA blogosphere goes beyond personal blogs and knowledge
sharing. More and more executives within the bank were becoming
interested in a fashionable concept in 2009—launching a BBVA-
branded mobile operator. Virgin Mobile is an example of this arrange-
ment, called an MVNO or mobile virtual network operator, in which a
company with a highly visible brand supplies the marketing while a
mobile operator like Sprint or O2 supplies the actual mobile and
billing infrastructure. BBVA created an internal shared blog around the
topic, with multiple contributors from a virtual team that spanned
geographies and included strategy and technology staff. By commenting on each other's posts, the working group surfaced issues and cited
information from elsewhere. This activity culminated in an in-person
workshop, where attendees familiar with the issues from each other's
blogging and commenting activity convened in one place.

In the end, BBVA decided the time was not right to move forward
with the MVNO, although they continue to collaborate to keep an eye
on this market. Their collaboration had revealed that the project, while
sexy, had significant drawbacks for now. Innovation is great. But collaboration, with the right tools, helps companies see better when a
HERO's innovation actually makes sense.

people and information: the two key sides of collaboration

HEROes work at the speed of empowered customers. They need tools that let them collaborate at the same speed.

In the HERO-powered business, speedy and effective collaboration is about finding people and information. The interesting thing about collaboration systems, like BBVA's blogosphere, is that workers use people to find information, and information to find people.

Carmen Benito is an interesting person. You might know her, or hear about her from other people at the bank. You might follow her blog because she and her perspective—and the unique way she expresses herself—interest you. By finding her, you learned about risk. You started with a person and ended up with information.

Another way people find information in collaboration systems is through search. If you are interested in risk, you can search BBVA's blogosphere and find Carmen's blog. Then you might find Carmen, and ask for her help. You started with information and it led you to a person. Search is key. As Fernando Summers explains, "The usefulness of the information lies in the ease of access. Searches must be high quality to give better access to the knowledge behind them . . . Otherwise, this collaboration becomes a source of information without added value."

But while the links between people and information are important elements in the design of a collaboration system, they're not the most important elements. In fact, what typically makes or breaks a collaboration system doesn't have to do with its design, or even its content. What makes the difference is the plan companies use to roll it out— the cultural elements and the HEROes who create it. That's the lesson to learn from IBM and its Blue IQ Ambassador program.

CASE STUDY

how social adoption helped IBM's Blue IQ catch on

In 2008, IBM Software Group senior vice president Steve Mills wanted to teach IBM's sales teams how to be more productive using collaboration tools. Salespeople were frustrated by how much time they spent seeking people and information. Some said they spent at least half their time just looking for stuff, searching for experts to put in front of clients, chasing down the answer to a client question, or locating the right information to complete and win a proposal. If the next salesperson needed similar information, she was stuck; the knowledge wasn't shared.

Steve hoped that IBM's own Lotus Connections product, an internal social network that includes profiles, blogs, comments, search tagging, wikis, activities, and microblogs, could solve the sales teams' problems. But salespeople are a hard audience to win over—they focus on immediate results. Steve gave Gina Poole the job of convincing the salespeople to use the sharing tools.

Gina was a good choice. She had spent over fifteen years in a passionate quest to help people at IBM to communicate and collaborate better. She pioneered IBM's Internet marketing in the 1990s, launching the developerWorks program, a community of a million or so developers centered around open standards technologies and IBM products. She launched "grass roots marketing," an early form of social media marketing, building relationships with external Web communities that drove 25 percent of developerWorks's traffic. And she ran IBM's University Ambassador program, in which thirty-five hundred IBM staffers volunteered their time in local universities and colleges. When Steve came to her with the challenge of winning over IBM salespeople to the new system, they decided to use the idea of ambassadors again, only this time within IBM instead of in universities. They christened the effort IBM's Blue IQ Ambassadors.

Gina's success came through a pyramid of people.

She started with six full-time Blue IQ staffers. She identified highly visible IBM bloggers and wiki volunteers, people who were backers of the new social tools and influential with other IBMers, and hired six of them. These six people would have to drive change through four hundred thousand employees at IBM. She knew they couldn't do it alone.

In the process of recruiting, though, she had turned up a hundred people who were fans of the new way of doing business. They became the core group as she built an ambassador program. She was seeking people who not only believed in the new tools, but intimately understood how IBM people did their jobs.

Then, with the help of the one hundred fans of the idea, she recruited twelve hundred Blue IQ volunteers from all functions in the company, all around the world, and asked them to be her ambassadors. Her hundred fans helped spread the word; she provided the ambassadors with motivation, recognition, and membership in an exclusive club. She empowered these ambassadors to help with recruitment and training of other sales staffers. Volunteers started with existing success stories, then added their own narratives of success. Gina's team provided a community, a place to share ideas, concerns, and success stories, tools to teach, and what Gina calls an Enablement Plan, a specific and tailored program of activities to bring a team along.

Finally, Gina implemented a program of "social adoption." Here's how it works. Her ambassadors, using training and materials from the Blue IQ program in fifty countries around the world, conduct one-on-one meetings to connect with IBM sales staff who are looking for help. Blue IQ ambassadors also host one-to-many Lunch & Learn sessions to bring local success stories into the light of day.

Driving social adoption also means doing internal consulting. The core team and some volunteers do what Gina calls a Blue IQ Jump-Start program, with Blue IQ Ambassadors serving as internal consultants to a sales or technical support team. After sitting with teams to understand what they are trying to accomplish, the ambassadors build an Enablement Plan with the most appropriate tools and activities. The ambassador then stays in touch with the team until the adoption is well under way. Now the team is another force for adoption of the program.

Gina keeps her ambassador volunteers motivated with awards and recognition. The ambassadors vote each quarter on the ten most valuable ambassadors, who then get a gift certificate, recognition, and a personal letter from Steve Mills. Gina also created an executive virtual forum so these winners can interact with IBM executives. Every ambassador gets visibility and experience and establishes him or herself as an expert in social media.

Did it work? IBM has accelerated its pace of sales productivity, innovation, and profitability. Profits were up in 2008 and 2009, two very tough years for the technology business. Productivity improvements like the Blue IQ Ambassador program helped.

Today, two-thirds of IBM staffers around the world use internal wikis, and the other tools are almost as popular. The cultural transformation of the sales organization, from information hoarders to information sharers, is well under way.

All it took was a pyramid of HEROes: one leader, six staffers, one hundred fans, twelve hundred ambassadors, four hundred thousand employees.

sharing systems need the right plan *and* the right execution

Your company may be very different from IBM, but if you've got at least two hundred people working with computers on their desks, you and IBM probably have more in common than you think.

Like IBM, your people are probably duplicating efforts and failing to get the most value they can from sharing information. Your HEROes may feel empowered, but they need resources to act. And while a system like IBM's Blue IQ can help, as you can see, it's not so easy to get people using it.

While intranets, SharePoint document repositories, and sharing systems are all the rage right now, collaboration systems often fail to attract workers. In fact, for every company we see with an active set of employees collaborating, there are three with dead, rarely used intranets. The IT department may put up a SharePoint server, then wonder why it isn't getting much use. Or there's an initial rush of interest around a project, but then it dies down.

The problem with collaboration systems and technologies, regardless of what form they come in, is not the technology. It's inertia. People like to keep doing things the same way they always have. For the most part, that means email. Email isn't a very good way to collaborate, and it's really poor at solving the obstacles that HEROes face as they build projects together, but email has inertia, and inertia is a powerful force.

For a collaboration system to transform the way people work—as Blue IQ did for IBM, and the internal blogosphere did for BBVA—it requires more than support from IT or a push from management. Both IT and management need to work to reduce the effort that workers must put in before they can use the system. Those workers need to see results quickly. And the system must be built to spread success rapidly. From observing hundreds of companies that have succeeded—and failed—at rolling out collaboration systems, we've identified five recommendations that can maximize your chances of success. They depend on culture at least as much as technology.

1. Build collaboration systems that extend existing tools.

2. Make sure anyone participating gets value instantly.

3. Dedicate people to the rollout.

4. Solve 80 percent of the problem, then stop and listen.

5. Build adoption socially and virally.

Let's take a look at each of these in context.

build collaboration systems that extend existing tools

Take a close look at the set of tools people are already using at your company. Your collaboration system must work with that.

For example, at BBVA, the blogosphere project followed an earlier project called Infobook, a repository of documents that people already used. It was also integrated with the work login and ID that BBVA employees already used.

Tools that connect with smartphones, enable simple photo uploads, or function like Facebook, Twitter, or Wikipedia tend to be popular. Anything complex enough to require an explanation is far less likely to succeed.

Of course, the most important element of extending existing tools is integration with email. Any tool that requires abandoning email will fail—instead, collaboration tools should work *with* emails, providing notifications when things get updated, as Yammer does.

And people in different groups need to use the same tools. If you want to avoid a Babel of incompatible tools just when things seem to be taking off, IT should standardize the sharing tools. For example, at Intel, different teams can use different tools—blogs, forums, wikis, and so on—but the IT group has ensured that they all work off the corporate directory and they all plug into the search engine. Because search and identity are standard, people from all around Intel can count on utility as they connect with the company's sharing tools, and on support when they build their own.[1]

make sure anyone participating gets value instantly

It's easy to see the value of collaboration systems once everyone is using them. But that's not how things get adopted. The complex "knowledge sharing systems" that preceded today's collaboration tools mostly failed, because their benefits became clear only after everyone had joined and contributed (the classic chicken-and-egg problem). Instead, individuals adopt the system one at a time; at first, only a minority will be using the system. It follows that each adopter should get value as soon as she signs up.

Remember, as you learn what this value is, to think about two kinds of people using the system: those *seeking* information and those *contributing* information. Both must get immediate benefits.

Seekers want information. Everybody who uses the Internet knows how to find things: search. So your information portal needs to have a search that's excellent, and works just like Google. To start, it helps if there's a core of information worth searching, like BBVA's Infobook.

The contributor's point of view is different. The contributor, like Carmen Benito at BBVA, wants to share information and insights. A site designed to encourage this sharing must make it dead easy to set up and share content. Setting up a blog at BBVA is as easy as setting up a blog on the open Internet. What kills these sites is approvals, or anything else that gets in the way of posting quickly. Sharing sites work best when the impulse to contribute leads immediately to a contribution.

Here's how this works at IBM. On the Blue IQ sharing site, it's easy to "tag" searches and content with relevant terms. This yields an immediate payoff for both types of contributors in searches. People who contribute content and tag it spread it more quickly by making it easier for others to find. And people seeking content are more likely to find what they're looking for. Result: one in five IBM employees now tag searches or content, because the payoff is immediate.

dedicate people to the rollout

As you saw from Gina Poole and Steve Mills at IBM, you don't get transformational benefits without spending money on people and programs to sell the initiative. The seven full-time staffers and twelve hundred volunteer ambassadors for Blue IQ are a lot of people to dedicate to social technology change management, but we've seen the same pattern at other companies—spreading HERO projects takes resources.

Amazingly, the best way to find resources may be to look at their activities on the open Internet. Sogeti is a technology services company based in Europe, with twenty thousand people in fifteen countries. Michiel Boreel, the CTO, found four hundred socially active employees around the world by looking for Sogeti mentions on Twitter, Facebook, and LinkedIn. When he wanted to launch TeamPark, an internal social technology platform built on IBM's Lotus Connections, he reached out to this group. Two hundred of them immediately volunteered and are now the core evangelists for social technology adoption inside of Sogeti.

Here's another example of how it takes people to spread technology inside an organization. David Michael is CIO of a business unit at London-based United Business Media Limited (UBM), a media company that publishes magazines, runs media Web sites like TechWeb, and puts on trade shows like the Enterprise 2.0 conferences. They write about social technologies—could they use them internally?

It sure looked like a slam dunk. "We built a secure wiki to support a CEO offsite where the CEOs of our independent business groups were getting together," David explains. "And they loved it. Social technology became a big theme of the offsite, to use it to cut across organizational boundaries and transform our business. For the first time, they had a place to go to get the same information at the same time and exchange ideas. It was a terrific thing."

But when UBM tried to expand this to the rest of the organization, with blogging, wiki, and community, it failed. "We had basically zero usage," David says. "It fell off a cliff."

David tried again. He changed the technology platform to Jive Software, because it included community features, not just a wiki. And he hired a full-time community manager named Ted Hopton. Now remember, most customer communities have community managers. But in our experience, most internal employee communities don't. That's part of why they don't catch on—nobody's responsible.

Ted applied his unique qualities to evangelizing the community. Not only did he know how UBM worked, he was "incredibly sociable, willing to pick up the phone and sell it to employees," as David describes. In Ted's words, "one-to-one conversation is so critical. If we can help just one person understand how to use the wiki and get excited about it, then they become an evangelist to spread the word throughout their division . . . I spend a lot of time answering inquiries and explaining."

David Levin, the company's CEO, was a supporter and made internal information sharing a corporate priority for 2010. And Ted made connections. As he says, "Every division head knows me. Usually they're happy to talk, but sometimes they'd rather not see me coming. They know I'm going to bug them to figure out how to make the wiki work in their business."

Word spread. Now UBM has hundreds of small communities and a dozen or so larger, business-transforming communities. The most active communities are ones involving technology change or business opportunity. For example, UBM is ramping up a new business hosting virtual events. This requires a lot of technology and a new business model, not to mention new ways of presenting content and driving attendance. The community of people with experience or interest inside UBM is helping to spread this to more parts of the company. Hiring Ted as community manager made all the difference.

solve 80 percent of the problem, then stop and listen

Shawn Dahlen learned this the hard way. Shawn is the social media program manager at defense company Lockheed Martin and the man behind the Unity project. He's a HERO who put together a case and initially received $5,000 in funding to demonstrate how social technology tools could help engineers and client teams within the company's Information Systems & Global Services (IS&GS) business area. (That initial business case has since spawned a system based on Microsoft SharePoint that supports the entire Lockheed Martin enterprise.)

What Shawn learned is simple. "You have to think big, but start small." At first, Shawn thought that his original vision for blogs and communities would work for everybody. But it didn't turn out that way. Not everybody wanted the cool extra features, and he realized a few things were missing. What Shawn and his team learned is that what worked for them didn't necessarily work for other groups. Instead, they had to put the basic tools out there and start groups on one project. Once that succeeded, they learned to listen to what people really needed and to incorporate feedback on the fly.

In Gina Poole's experience at IBM, "solve 80 percent, then stop and listen" meant introducing the capabilities, then listening carefully for what people are trying to accomplish, then showing them how the capabilities can help and getting immediate feedback. By applying this principle, her ambassadors have even brought ideas for new features like shared files back to the Lotus Connections product team.

build adoption socially and virally

Any useful collaboration system has features that allow those who love it to spread it easily. Like viral marketing outside the firewall, collaboration and innovation systems need viral elements that work within companies. The sequence is simple: I use it, I like it, I tell others, they sign up, they use it, they like it, and so on.

The simplest features of this kind integrate with emails. For example, Chubb's Imaginatik application, described in the previous chapter, included a feature that would allow people to forward innovation ideas to others for review. This generated immediate interest from people who might not have heard about the innovation contest before. Deloitte Australia's Yammer application can send updates and digests through email as well.

At Sun Life, the Canadian financial services company, two senior managers used a different tool from the groundswell: viral video. The VP of market development and the SVP for group benefits created a video with themselves as avatars explaining an idea contest to get people excited. The video spread rapidly and generated a rapid increase in participation. Around twenty-seven hundred employees participated and generated more than two hundred fifty ideas.

And at one pharmaceutical company we worked with, the company built the training materials for the sharing system right into the sharing tool. Twenty people worked on the rollout, which had to succeed where previous global knowledge management tools had failed. The team made learning about the new tools a priority, both with formal classroom sessions and distance learning options and a complete syllabus of instructions only a click away. With the teaching tools embedded into the platform, people will be able to support themselves and each other by sending links to the appropriate place.

management and IT must combine to support HEROes

In the previous chapter and this one, we showed how management and IT can live up to one part of the HERO Compact: providing resources to support HEROes. Systems that stimulate innovation and collaboration are important for two reasons: they help HEROes go from ideas to projects to successes, and even more importantly, they demonstrate that the company values HERO-driven innovation.

As you've seen in the last two chapters, these systems don't always work. Forrester analyst Rob Koplowitz, who has seen many of these deployments, explains: "The dream of Enterprise 2.0 is just that—a dream—unless companies can get people participating. IT support is not sufficient—we've heard too many stories from IT professionals who described projects' failure to launch." Management support is not sufficient either—an edict from the top to "collaborate more" or "use the new system" won't make much difference. But when IT and management build and support a system together, HEROes are far more likely to participate.

Collaboration systems are just one place where projects can succeed only if IT participates, rather than blocking a project. In fact, in any do-it-yourself HERO projects, the potential for conflict escalates because they include technologies that, historically, the IT department has controlled.

In the HERO-powered business, this just won't fly. IT must recognize it has a new job here—supporting these projects as a technology advisor and helping HEROes to manage risks, even when the IT department is not in control. In the next two chapters, we describe how IT can keep HEROes and their projects safe and secure, and how it can support HEROes' projects.

12. keeping HEROes safe

It's time to face the risks that lurk in the HERO-powered business. Because employees, armed with the technologies of the groundswell, are not just powerful, they're dangerous. Like all powerful tools, these technologies carry risks.

What could go wrong?

For one thing, as Domino's Pizza found out in April of 2009, employees can upload videos to YouTube. In this case, it was two pizza makers stuffing cheese up their noses and performing other unspeakable acts on food that appeared destined for delivery to customers. No matter that the perpetrators eventually denied ever delivering unsanitary food, Domino's still suffered brand damage.[1]

Your employees don't do that? What about the Sprint employee who posted details about the Palm Pre phone on a blog, violating a nondisclosure agreement?[2]

And it's not just malicious employees. At Cisco, an employee posted a job opening, inadvertently revealing a change in strategic direction. At Microsoft, a product manager announced he was changing jobs, revealing the unannounced news that a product was being discontinued.

And we haven't even gotten to security breaches. An employee at a global bank just told us that, unable to remember the passwords to the twelve corporate systems he used, he wrote them all down on a piece of paper taped to his laptop.

Employees are a danger to themselves and their companies because they use whatever technology they can get their hands on. This technology has potential risks. So how can you lock down technology to keep them from doing any of these things?

You can't.

There was a time years ago when IT security meant locking down your network and corporate databases, putting everything behind the drawbridge and moat that protect the corporate castle, and giving only authorized people the password. Secrets were safe. Well, mostly safe.

But now the communication tools are wherever your employees are. Responding to customers at the speed of the groundswell, HEROes in your company use email, instant messages, blogs, blog comments, Facebook, LinkedIn, Twitter, YouTube, Flickr, Skype, WebEx, Google Docs, YouSendIt, and hundreds of other sites and tools, more every day. They work, not just on corporate PCs, but on their own computers, iPhones, BlackBerry phones, and tablet PCs. As we saw in chapter 7, over 40 percent of information workers are provisioning their own technology. How are you supposed to lock all this down? One IT security professional described his job to us as "a world gone mad."

You can't protect things any more by locking down the network and password-protecting the databases. While IT was busy securing the network perimeter to keep secrets inside and intruders outside, the perimeter moved. It moved to wherever an employee is trying to work.

It's as if you had built a giant fortress to protect your village from marauders only to wake up one morning and find that the villagers had moved all their houses into the fields beyond the safety of the fortress. They won't come back in where it's safe. It doesn't suit their needs. It makes getting things done too slow and it prevents them from working in the ways they need. They like it out in the fields.

Malcolm Harkins has a great way to describe this. As Intel's chief information security officer, he's responsible for keeping the company's secrets and people safe. At his first security team meeting in 2005, his team was complaining that the security perimeter had vanished. Securing the corporate network was no longer enough to protect the company. But Malcolm saw it differently. He saw that the perimeter hadn't vanished, "it had moved and we just missed it."

You can't lock all this stuff down. The more you try, the more you slow down and trip up the HEROes. You need a new IT security strategy. And just like your customer strategy, you're going to have to depend on the one thing you have going for you—the intelligence of your workforce. Or as Malcolm Harkins says, "Make people the new perimeter."

the new job of information security

Remember the HERO Compact? In it, we said that the HEROes' job is, in part, to obey the rules set up by the IT group to keep them safe.

Since locking down technology doesn't work so well, the parts of IT that focus on security must focus more of their efforts on policy and education and risk. IT has two new jobs:

1. Train and educate information workers about how to keep themselves safe.

2. Help HEROes assess, manage, and mitigate risks associated with their projects.

Note what's not included here. IT is not *responsible* for risk. Instead, people in IT must advise workers to keep them safe, and help them to improve the security of what they do.

CASE STUDY

making Kodak's HEROes safer

Bruce Jones knows about risk. Bruce has global responsibility for IT, security, forensics, compliance, data privacy, and risk management at Kodak. As an IT security professional, Bruce has been dealing with the risks that come with new technology at Kodak for twenty-nine years.

Managing risk is in Bruce's background. He comes from a law enforcement family. His father and grandfather served and protected their communities going back to the 1930s. Risk and safety and bad guys were everyday topics of conversation.

But Kodak is a business, and if Kodak isn't making money, there's nothing to keep safe. In the past five years, Kodak has had its share of not making money as its film business has declined with the relentless rise of digital cameras. That gives Bruce a lot of motivation to help the business grow.

One way Kodak grows is to get closer to customers. After all, Kodak was built on empowered customers, people capturing their Kodak moments and making memories part of their lives. Photo sharing has become a killer application for Facebook and, increasingly, for Twitter.

Kodak's employee HEROes have embraced the groundswell and become active participants in the customer conversation, listening to rebukes, responding to concerns, reaching out to its customers. Kodak's Facebook pages from around the world are swamped with fans and with Kodak employees. Kodak's YouTube videos are viral and touching. Kodak's Twitter presence advertises product deals and tips for photographers. Kodak's employees are everywhere online, talking about Kodak.

This activity creates risks. In the spring of 2009, Bruce noticed an alarming increase in email spam on Kodak's corporate systems, from around 8 million to 58 million messages a month. Kodak's spam filters blocked most of it, but the spam filters were overloaded and valuable business messages were delayed. Why? Bruce attributes a large portion of the increase in spam to company employees who had posted their Kodak email addresses in places where spammers could find them, including in social networks. Then Kodak increased its visibility through its sponsorship and product placement within the popular program *Celebrity Apprentice* on NBC. While this created a lot of buzz about Kodak, it also attracted spammers, who then noticed all those highly visible Kodak email addresses.

Spam is no joke—many spam messages include links that invite email recipients to sites filled with viruses and other malware. In the past, the typical response would have been an attempt to further lock down corporate systems to keep the bad stuff out. Instead, Bruce decided to work on educating Kodak's staff, to make them as smart as possible in a dangerous online world. He moved the perimeter.

Bruce started with a new policy to protect employees engaged in social media inside and outside the company. Bruce joined a cross-functional team from Kodak's legal, security, marketing, and corporate communications departments to create a simple pamphlet called "Social Media Tips: Sharing lessons learned to help your business grow." The content included perspectives and policies from human resources, IT, and marketing; you can read it at Kodak.com.[3] They also created a more specific version for internal use at Kodak. In Bruce's words, "We spent the most time deciding how to make this applicable to everybody." They kept it simple, to get as many people as possible to read it. The objective was to improve online safety through education.

The guidelines in these policies include things like "Know what you are talking about," "Always be transparent," and "Listen to what others have to say." But along with these simple, friendly, helpful tips are important policies: no anonymous posts or comments, don't talk about things you shouldn't, accept personal responsibility when you make a mistake. The tips apply to internal and external communications. And while they are written for social media, they apply equally well to video, cloud computing services, and mobile communications—all the technologies of the groundswell.

The social media tips pamphlet is written in English, but deployed globally and available to the public. There's also a forty-minute self-guided course on security awareness that now includes social media guidance in sixteen languages. Each employee takes the course every other year as part of the business conduct policy.

By educating the staff on where the guardrails are in social environments, Bruce changed the way Kodak thinks about technology. Now maybe they won't post their Kodak email addresses in places where they shouldn't. But more importantly, Bruce helped Kodak communicate the message: "We trust you and we'd like to keep you safe." He showed the employees how to be safe. That's a much better message than "We're worried you will screw up so we are locking you down."

Instead of locking Kodak staff out of social environments, they are now free to reach out and interact with customers and friends there. Kodak needs this flexibility to continue building its brand. A company transforming itself—like Kodak's transition to a postfilm world—needs all the employee HEROes it can get with creative ideas to help with that transformation. Kodak's policies encourage HEROes to innovate safely.

Bruce sees his job now as helping these HEROes. He anticipates technologically dangerous events and educates employees and managers on the potential risks of the business initiatives they come up with, particularly those involving groundswell technologies: employees using social media, smartphones, and cloud Internet services. It's not his job to say no to a HERO project. It's his job to say, "Here are some potential consequences. Here are the risks we may face in doing this, and *here's what we can do about it.*"

policies and education help protect HEROes and their employers

Kodak is just one example of a company that's using policies, education, and training to keep HEROes safe as they engage in the groundswell. So have BBVA, Boeing, Booz Allen Hamilton, Electronic Arts, IBM, Intel, Lockheed Martin, Procter & Gamble, and Verizon. These policies vary, but they include three foundational principles of groundswell safety. These principles are deceptively simple, but each has a track record of success. You can write them on a notecard (see table 12-1):

1. Put your name on everything you do.

2. Remember that you are an employee.

3. Own up to mistakes and fix them.

put your name on everything you do

We get this question more than any other: "Should we require a login for internal social applications?" The answer is always yes, because the first principle is to make employees use their real names and identities. Anonymous contributions undermine the balance between employees and management that's fundamental to the HERO Compact. Employees will watch their words if they know those words can be traced back to them. At Electronic Arts, Bert Sandie, the director of

TABLE 12-1

Principles of groundswell safety

Principle	What it means for employees	What it means for employers
Put your name on everything you do.	Do not post or comment or tweet anonymously. Everything carries your name on it, which means you are responsible for what you say and do. Be careful.	Employees need a single identity for all their internal activities. Then you can worry less about inappropriate or business-risky communications.
Remember that you are an employee.	Don't act as an individual while on company time or when dealing with company matters. Act as a representative of the company. Be honest, but be respectful.	Your business conduct policy should set the right expectations for employees. New tools don't change the rules of conduct. If an employee violates a policy, that's a personnel issue, not an IT issue.
Own up to mistakes and fix them.	You will make mistakes. Before you post, ask yourself if you would be proud showing it to your mother. If you make a mistake, remember that your name is on it. Reach out and deal with repercussions. Be courageous. As a result, you will earn trust and goodwill.	As with any situation, employees will make mistakes. Treat them as learning and development opportunities. Build an environment of trust and "I've got your back."

technical excellence at EA University, says that this policy of requiring a login and identity has resulted in exactly zero posts or comments that had to be taken down. Fernando Summers at BBVA said once this policy went into effect, there were no problems on the company's internal blogosphere.

The first principle—identify yourself—applies both to employees working internally and to those working externally. Internally, it's generally straightforward to require a user name and password and include the employee's name (and in best practice, their picture) on every profile, blog post, internal cloud service, and comment. To make it easier for employees (which will encourage participation), this means moving toward an architecture where a single login provides access to all the applications an employee needs, including social, video, and cloud applications.

Externally, this transparency principle must be implemented as policy, which is what Kodak does. At Best Buy, as we described in chapter 1, retail store employees can join the Twelpforce and answer questions on Twitter. But they must first register their handle with Twelpforce. IBM's social computing guidelines include this statement:[4]

> Identify yourself—name and, when relevant, role at IBM—when you discuss IBM or IBM-related matters. And write in the first person. You must make it clear that you are speaking for yourself and not on behalf of IBM.

remember that you are an employee

This principle is a reminder that while groundswell technologies provide new ways to communicate, collaborate, and publish, they don't actually change any of the responsibilities that you already have as an employee.

At IBM, this principle is reinforced in the social computing policy and in a direct reference to its Business Conduct Guidelines, also available publicly on IBM.com in the Investors/Corporate Governance section. At Sun Life Financial, a Canada-based financial services company, this principle is anchored in the employee code of conduct and made visible in the social media guidelines.

Oddly, this is the place where most businesses have abdicated responsibility to the IT security organization. The sentiment seems to be, "If it involves technology, it must be an IT policing job to keep people from doing the wrong thing." That's ludicrous. If an employee is going to violate a corporate policy or break the law, that's a personnel issue, not an IT issue. It's a business responsibility. Breaking that law or violating that policy on a public site like Facebook, Twitter, or a blog doesn't change that responsibility at all.

So this principle exists for one purpose only: to remind employees that they are first and foremost an employee when acting on company time or on company business. This doesn't apply specifically to groundswell technology, either. It could happen in person, by phone, or through email. The principle serves to remind employees whom they're working for and what their responsibilities are. If Domino's staff had known more about this principle, maybe they wouldn't have posted that damaging video on YouTube.

own up to mistakes and fix them

This last principle is more human than the others. It recognizes that we aren't perfect. We might be grumpy some day and snipe at a customer rather than address their concerns. Or post while venting anger rather than after taking a walk to calm down.

This principle has two main components. First, it tells an employee that it's okay to make mistakes as long as you do everything in your power to fix them. If a post has a fact wrong, then fix it with a crossout and the correct information. If a tweet kicks off a firestorm of angry responses, then tweet back and apologize and offer to make it good. It's the employee version of what Domino CEO Patrick Doyle did after the video incident. He apologized publicly and with visible emotion on YouTube. It's a mea culpa, and it's okay as long as you make good.

The second component is more subtle. It says that employers must trust and support employee HEROes. While this will always be a judgment call, the right posture is to help the employee work through the mistake and make it right. Firing them is usually the wrong approach. And even when things seem to go wrong on a project, it's often more productive to fix it than to pull the plug.

This principle also means that managers need to show faith in employees rather than shutting them down at the first sign of problems. Here's an example from IBM. In 2007, CEO Sam Palmisano approved using IBM's Innovation Jam system to ask employees for suggestions on how to improve the company. At the end of the first day, the jam was full of complaints, not suggestions. Sam resisted the temptation to shut it down immediately as a failure, because he had faith in the company's employees to contribute appropriately. Sure enough, by the second day, the complaints petered out and the suggestions started to appear. By day three, the suggestions were coming in full bore and the complaints were few and far between.

Now IBM's Innovation Jams are frequent and productive—and the management is glad they didn't pull the plug. And as a helpful "I've got your back" by-product of this experience, Sam Palmisano reads every idea post and has made some organizational changes based on the feedback, positive and negative, without any retribution.

Empowered employees make mistakes. Punishing them sends the message that innovation is a career risk. Management's job is to get employees' actions and self-interest aligned with company goals. If not, then you have a much bigger problem to solve than information security; you have a workforce that operates in fear. That's not good for generating employee HEROes.

assessing, managing, and mitigating risk

From Kodak and IBM, we've seen the principles involved in using policy, education, and training to help with risk. We said this was the first of the two new jobs of IT security. The second is helping HEROes to assess, manage, and mitigate risks. IT people must advise those building with technology on what might go wrong, and what alternatives might be better.

Bruce Jones at Kodak does this. "I'll tell you the risks and the likelihood that the risk will happen, and I'll work with you to understand the potential business impact," he says. "But at the end of the day, it's a business decision. Our job is to assess and help manage the risk. Your job is to run the business."

Bruce's team manages this risk assessment process, but the business leader signs off on it. Kodak uses a multitier approach, where general managers or other senior leaders approve riskier initiatives and local managers approve smaller projects. But the focus is still on people to manage risks, not technology to lock everything down.

Again, as with policy and education, the focus is on people, not just systems. As Khalid Kark, Forrester's expert on security, puts it, "You have to start where the information is, and that's wherever your people are. It requires rethinking your security architecture." Instead of a locked-down network, the new security architecture has three layers: people, risk assessment, and information protection.

1. *Build systems that recognize that people are the new perimeter.* As Malcolm Harkins of Intel says, "The perimeter is anywhere your people are, from an application developer who left in a buffer overflow to an employee that clicks on a blog link that leads to a malware Web site. Our job is to help each person on the perimeter to understand where they stand and how to be aware of potential danger."

2. *Give those people tools to manage risk.* This starts with an IT-led security assessment: How dangerous is it? How likely is it to occur? Then an authorized business manager makes the decision, as at Kodak. Dell's Manish Mehta, whom we described in chapter 9, helps Dell's HEROes building social applications with best practices for safe social interactions. The chief information security officer in IT must work with HR, legal, compliance, and the business sponsor to make sure any business decision is made with full knowledge of the risks. But ultimately, it's a business decision, not an IT decision.

3. *Use technology that protects information, not just networks.* Traditional security technology secures the network. In a new job for IT, the new security technology must protect information, particularly applications and Web access. It must also deal with new devices, cloud computing services, a mobile and remote workforce, new media types like video, and new channels of communication like Facebook and Twitter. The security team will have to invest in technologies like data-loss protection technology from vendors like Symantec and McAfee that keep confidential information such as customer social security numbers from showing up in email messages. It will have to look into new message-interception technology from start-ups like Socialware to allow employees to use Facebook and Twitter to answer customer questions while remaining in compliance with regulations.

This new security architecture frees the IT department from a no-win task. IT security has for too long been the department of "no," the group that told business HEROes what not to do. Now it can be the department of "yes, and here's how." IT goes from policing to working with legal, HR, and business owners in assessing, managing, and mitigating risk, and matching it up with value.

when to say no to a HERO

We're not naive. There are still times when you and your IT security team and legal staff must say no to an employee HERO, when her actions are just too dangerous to continue. But the goal should always be to analyze the real risks so that eventually you can say yes.

For example, the rules around customer communications in the U.S. financial industry now require archiving and retaining sales employees' tweets and Facebook updates. So, until IT can find and implement a solution to intercept and archive the messages, banks are right to ban these activities for sales and service people for customer messages, until interception and archiving solutions become available.

Here are four situations where you should probably just say no:

- *When your regulator has created new laws that you can't yet comply with.* This applies to many banking, brokerage, and insurance applications, as well as applications in some life sciences companies. It doesn't mean shutting down internal deployments of social technology or cloud computing, but it does make external applications more complex.

- *When your customer contracts prevent you from sharing anything about the contract.* This applies to external communications for the defense industry. Building a secure collaboration platform for you and your customer to use is okay, and may even be required. Internal social applications are fine. But employees must be highly aware of laws banning the export of intellectual property and sharing customer secrets.

- *When your legal team has issued an opinion that prevents it.* This often happens when the legal team hasn't yet figured out the legal risks. For example, are video conferences "electronic communications" like emails that have to be archived? Or are they "voice communications" like phone calls that don't? The U.S. law hasn't decided, but you must. Your legal team is responsible for keeping the company—and you—out of court. Listen to them, but also make them part of your policy team.

- *When your HERO could be compromising customer or employee data.* Privacy laws in the United States and especially in Europe and some Asian countries make it clear when any information about an employee or consumer must be protected. Here, you can get to yes, but it's even more important to set up and train people on the principles.

how IT goes from prevention to support

In the HERO Compact, IT's job does not end with keeping HEROes safe. The IT group must also shift its responsibility to making HEROes successful. This is how IT goes from the department of "no" to the department of "yes"—and it's how HEROes go from supporting players to a force for innovation within companies. We describe all of that in chapter 13.

13. supporting HEROes with technology innovation

Gerald Shields is an insatiably curious chief information officer; he reads fifty books a year. He's always looking for the next big idea, the new important thing around the next corner. That curiosity has paid off for Gerald's employer, Aflac.

Aflac is a supplemental insurance company, memorable for its talking duck and the wise words of spokesperson Yogi Berra. A lot of people interact with Aflac. Eighty thousand licensed agents sell its products to employers. The company works with four hundred thousand payroll and benefits administrators who serve 50 million individual policyholders.

In 2008, Gerald decided that what was around the next corner was social technology and communities.

Most CIOs don't think about stuff like this. Gerald's day job is to manage six hundred IT professionals and a $135 million budget. His people operate the systems that keep Aflac's transactions flowing and the networks that bind the company together. They are responsible for keeping Aflac safe from bad-guy attacks on customer data and in compliance with regulations. And he's good at it; he was on *CIO Magazine*'s Top 100 CIOs list in 2006 *and* 2008.

But in addition to running these systems, Gerald feels it's his job to show other executives the power that technology has to serve customers, starting with social technologies. Here's how he did it.

First he educated his direct reports and Paul Amos, Aflac's North American president and the grandson of the company's founder. Having convinced Paul, he began to work with the new CMO, Jeff Charney. Paul convened managers from all over the company for a workshop on social technologies. Cross-functional groups developed plans, which went through a rigorous review.

Out of those reviews, Jeff and Gerald selected the two most promising ideas and built communities with technology from community vendor Lithium. The first was a community site for the independent sales associates called The Buzz. With eighty thousand field people selling thousands of deals per month, it's important to give these independent agents a way to connect to each other and to their sales, service, and marketing support teams. On The Buzz, they can get and share information and help, exchange views and experiences, and interact with Aflac executives, including the head of customer service and Gerald. Each month, twenty-eight hundred associates visit or make a contribution.

The second community, called Duck Pond, serves Aflac's two hundred thousand online billing and payroll administrator customers in the United States. Payroll administrators are a group that needs friends, since they typically slave away in human resources or finance with few internal peers. Duck Pond helps these professionals connect and share their experiences and concerns, Aflac-related or not. For Aflac, Duck Pond is a great way to serve these customers while building loyalty. In Gerald's words, "We don't want you to think of Aflac as just a supplemental insurance company. We want you to say, 'Wait a minute. I'm on Duck Pond all the time.'"

Gerald's teams still have their hands full running the systems that keep Aflac's transactions flowing and operations humming, keeping the company out of court and in compliance with regulations, and running a big technology operation. But Gerald has made Aflac better by supporting technology innovation throughout the company.

If you're in IT, you could spend all your time running the core systems, locking down networks, and focusing on cutting costs just to return money to the bottom line. Or, like Gerald, you could do those things while keeping an eye on new technology and how it might be used to solve customer problems. You could become a key partner and advisor to customer-facing business functions. You could bring professional technology guidance to the HEROes throughout your company and watch innovation grow.

IT professionals and HERO employees share responsibility for business technology

HEROes build technology solutions, often on their own. So who needs IT?

The whole business does. Because while IT won't necessarily own the technology, it certainly can help make it better.

We've already seen how IT is keeping HEROes and the business safe by managing risk at Kodak and Intel. We saw how IT is helping businesspeople connect with social collaboration tools at United Business Media and IBM. And we learned how IT is supporting business innovation efforts at Chubb and Deloitte Australia.

IT also helps make HERO projects better. At PTC and Thomson Reuters, the projects moved forward more effectively with IT's help. And IT helps develop mobile applications that empower salespeople and customers, as we saw at Sunbelt Rentals and E*TRADE.

Building and operating business-grade technology, particularly in a company with more than a few hundred employees, requires specialized tools and specialty skills. Groundswell technology doesn't change that. Making a HERO solution work at business scale takes an IT organization. You wouldn't ask a HERO to manage the servers or run the compliance system or worry about the network bandwidth needs. That's IT's job.

While HEROes' technology ideas are customer focused, they aren't always business ready. IT's technology ideas are business ready but not always customer focused. But HEROes and IT working together can create business technology solutions that are customer focused *and* business ready. It takes a partnership between IT and HEROes to do it. That's the HERO Compact.

To see how this works, we'll take another look at Twelpforce, Best Buy's Twitter support system from chapter 1, to see how a technology staffer helped turn a HERO's idea into a success.

the technology story behind Best Buy's Twelpforce

As we described in chapter 1, it took a team to get Twelpforce off the ground, including CMO Barry Judge, Blue Shirt Nation cobuilder Gary Koelling, and marketing staffer John Bernier. But the technology *worked* because of an idea from Best Buy Web strategist/architect Ben Hedrington. These four employees are a living, breathing example of the Hero Compact—managers, marketers, and IT working together. Here's the technology back story of Twelpforce.

Behind Twelpforce, Best Buy's official Twitter customer service handle, are twenty-five hundred Best Buy retail staff employees plus a handful of customer service professionals. Each of these employees is empowered to tweet answers to customer questions, just as they do in person thousands of times a day in the retail stores. These tweets are tracked and redistributed through the Twelpforce Twitter handle.

Behind the Twitter handle was Ben's technology idea.

Ben's idea was building an experimental Twitter aggregation service called ConnectTweet.[1] This service, which runs silently and efficiently on Google's App Engine cloud servers, does a simple job. It uses Twitter's APIs (application programming interfaces) to continually search for Twitter posts with a defined hashtag ("Twelpforce," for example) and then repost them through a common Twitter ID.

Ben built ConnectTweet on his own time, as he put it, "after 5 p.m. every day for a week." The key ingredients were his own programming skills and a credit card to cover the cost of renting Google's servers. He coded directly on the Google cloud. Ben proved that it could work and opened it up, eventually, to several hundred kindred HEROes in other companies.

When Barry Judge, Gary Koelling, John Bernier, and Ben Hedrington decided to make this part of Best Buy's business, it took a month

and some contract developers with Python programming skills to create a business-ready version of ConnectTweet, still running on the
Google App Engine cloud.

With the trust embodied in the HERO Compact as the guiding
principle, it wasn't hard to do. Previous experience with Blue Shirt
Nation had laid the groundwork so Barry Judge and IT could see what
kinds of things were possible. So they opened up the corporate directory to Google's App Engine cloud and turned Twelpforce into a
business-ready customer solution.

The key lesson here is that when a HERO wants to move, IT must
be ready to move quickly to help. But how? By getting much closer to
HEROes and the technology they need to solve customer problems.

IT professionals have a new job: growing the business by supporting HEROes

At Forrester, we work with IT professionals who are supporting
HERO projects all the time. Based on these conversations, we have
identified four initiatives that CIOs and the IT organization can take
to support HEROes:

1. Create a cross-functional council to manage groundswell
    technologies.

2. Manage collaboration programs as part of the Information
    Workplace.

3. Research and implement technologies that anchor HERO
    solutions.

4. Build a portfolio of cloud services to accelerate HERO projects.

create a cross-functional council to manage groundswell technologies

To manage the do-it-yourself technology that employees are using, IT
should charter a new team of IT, business managers, and HEROes as a
cross-function groundswell technology council. This team tracks and
recommends technologies that employees are harnessing for work.

More than one third of employees are using do-it-yourself groundswell technologies. We've been analyzing this "consumerization of IT" since 2008.[2] In chapter 7, we explained why IT departments shouldn't block it when HEROes adopt groundswell technologies they learn about from their experience as consumers. But IT needs to go further, not just by getting out of the way, but by leading—educating and helping people in business functions to find these new technologies, helping them to see what's possible, and supporting what they come up with.

In chapter 9, we described how councils of people using similar technologies were effective in spreading best practices at Dell. The solution here is similar. IT should organize a new cross-functional advisory group with IT, HEROes, and managers. We call this a groundswell technology council.

The purpose of the council is to track and recommend groundswell technologies that the company can support and HEROes can adopt (see table 13-1). Manish Mehta's social strategy council at Dell, Michiel Boreel's TeamPark collaboration platform at Sogeti, and United Business Media's collaboration program are all instances of this idea. We've seen customers in the defense, consumer products, insurance, and life sciences industries use councils to analyze and select mobile and social technologies based on employee demand. The council basically helps the company and the workers to see where the promising technologies are, and how to support them.

For example, Dave Diedrich is vice president of technology, security, and workplace services and a twenty-five-year veteran at Kraft Foods. Dave started down the path to create a groundswell technology council when he decided to give employees a choice of smartphones and PDAs.[3] In his words, "We set out to see how we as an IT group could help Kraft Foods change the culture and contemporize the brand for employees."

The focus for Dave and his team was to get corporate email and collaboration capabilities on iPhones, which at the time were just gearing up to be viable in the business world. Dave got Kraft Foods into Apple's iPhone beta process for enterprise email support in 2008. Based on this experience, Dave was able to support iPhone use at the company, allowing employees to choose the iPhone as their personal device with access to work email and corporate applications beginning in the

TABLE 13-1

The groundswell technology council is a new cross-functional advisory group

Characteristics of the groundswell technology council	Description
Goal	Bring HEROes, IT professionals, and managers together to identify and prioritize the technologies that employees are harnessing to solve customer problems and get work done.
Mission	Advise the CIO and business managers on which do-it-yourself technologies to adopt and support. Test and implement alternatives to recommend specific vendors and solutions.
Council activities	Survey employees to determine their needs and technologies, prioritize initiatives based on data, work with IT to test alternatives, and make recommendations to IT and business.
IT's role	IT professionals organize, fund, and sponsor the council and are active participants providing technology guidance, highlighting opportunities and risks, and selecting platforms.
HEROes' role	HEROes identify the business opportunity and the potential solutions. They find others working on the same problem, connect to share experiences, and prioritize the needs.
Managers' role	Managers look for cross-departmental best practices and spur IT to research new technologies that look promising.

summer of 2008. The payoff has been big. In the words of one happy employee, "Thank you. You made me cool with my kids again." Another said, "I had everybody at the table jealous that my company lets me use an iPhone."

By working closely with employees and providing the security and business-ready capabilities that IT is good at, Dave and his team support, rather than block, grateful employees. Dave hopes to extend this initiative to cover other employee-provisioned technology as well.

manage collaboration programs as part of the Information Workplace

In chapter 11, we heard from Fernando Summers at BBVA about using collaboration technology to improve the flow of information and pace of teamwork. Collaboration is a business strategy—a way to improve the productivity of people and teams and accelerate the flow of information throughout the company. Because collaboration tools are technology deployed across every business and to every employee, IT should own the collaboration program.[4] IT will have to do two things to manage it.

First, the successful collaboration programs that we've seen have a unique leader behind them: a business executive with technology skills or a technology executive with business skills. Bill McCollam, vice president of digital strategy in the financial services company Sun Life, is a good example of this profile. He understands the technology so he can lead the charge, but he also understands what managers and employees in various departments worldwide need from a collaboration toolkit. By linking the technology with the business needs, he can tailor the program to the business.

Second, a collaboration program requires knitting together varied collaboration tools, information resources, and work and productivity applications and delivering them to an employee as a simple but comprehensive tool that we call the Information Workplace (see figure 13-1). The Information Workplace is valuable to employees because it ties together the tools each employee needs. Result: it's easy to move from email to wiki to instant message to Web conference to social network without having to switch tools or lose the context of what you're working on. Information Workplaces make people and teams more productive.

A fully formed Information Workplace is still a ways off for most companies because it's not yet possible to buy one from a single vendor. Even if it were, IT would have to stitch it into existing resources and deploy it globally. But over the past two years, companies including Verizon and Cisco have begun piecing the parts together to deliver a first-generation Information Workplace within their companies.

Some big vendors, including Cisco, Google, IBM, Microsoft, and Oracle, see this as a big opportunity to sell more solutions, so each is working hard to put the pieces together into a collaboration platform that can deliver an Information Workplace experience to every employee. While we expect advances in these platforms, don't hold your breath: it's better to get started helping employees to collaborate and get access to the best information now.

FIGURE 13-1

The Information Workplace is an integrated toolkit for employees

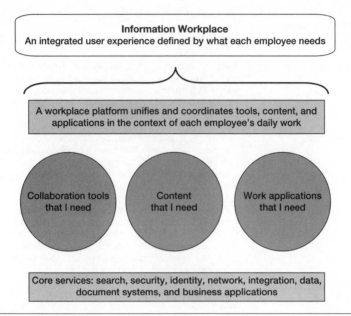

research and implement technologies that anchor HERO solutions

HERO projects require a new set of core technologies that many IT shops have yet to master. We have identified five anchor technologies that power many HERO projects[5] (see table 13-2).

1. *Deploy business analytics to make sense of all the new customer data.* The massive amount of data coming in over Twitter, customer communities, video views, and mobile Web site traffic is just so much clutter if it isn't measured and analyzed to find the meaning behind the clicks. This requires a new set of business intelligence and data-quality tools.[6]

2. *Master mobile technologies to build mobile applications.* But which ones? To reach the vast and growing diversity of smartphones, IT must make a bet on a mobile technology. Five different mobile operating systems compete for dominance, which makes building a native mobile application for all phones an

TABLE 13-2

New core technologies anchor HERO projects

Anchor technologies for HERO projects	Description
Business analytics	These tools help IT shops gather and report on customer data, mine Web and mobile click streams to find new marketing opportunities, and bring data dashboards to make information relevant and available to business managers and HEROes.
Mobile platforms	Five incompatible operating systems from Apple, Google, Microsoft, Nokia, and RIM make it tough to build one app for all smartphones. A promising new technology called HTML5 is challenging Flash and native apps to give developers a single mobile platform to target.
Social technology platforms	Enterprise 2.0 applications like wikis, blogs, and social networks are actually all just features in a social technology platform. IT should settle on a platform from a company like Cisco, IBM, Microsoft, or Jive Software to handle internal and some external situations, then fill in the missing pieces with start-ups.
Cloud APIs	Build cloud APIs to make cloud services part of the HERO toolkit while keeping the security, compliance, and data integration aspects in check. These APIs require native Internet technologies known as RESTful interfaces, as well as a secure link between your core systems and the cloud service.
New security infrastructure	To open doors to new HERO applications, IT must authenticate employees against the corporate directory, keep an eye on information flowing out to make sure it doesn't include confidential information, and archive customer communications to remain in compliance. This requires a new set of security services.

impossible task for most companies.[7] Currently, iPhone apps are setting the pace, but a big battle is shaping up between Adobe's Flash technology and an emerging standard called HTML5 for mobile applications that will run on most or all smartphones.

3. *Choose social technology platforms to support customer and employee communities.* Building communities takes an application or service. The market for customer communities is developing rapidly with over fifty vendors competing, led in our 2009 evaluation by

Jive Software and Teligent.[8] These solutions, as well as products by IBM and Microsoft, can work for employees. IT should take the lead on sussing out and testing the competing solutions for internal and external communities.

4. *Build cloud APIs to link internal security and data systems to cloud services.* For example, Ross Inglis at Thomson Reuters needed a way to get data out to the new independent financial advisor channel, and his IT team provided the APIs to do it. Interface technology is changing rapidly as a new set of tools called RESTful APIs are replacing older-style Web service interfaces.[9]

5. *Manage security as a business service.* We saw in chapter 12 that IT security needs an overhaul to deal with HERO employees and ever-expanding customer channels. Overhauling the security architecture will be difficult and costly, but will pay off in being able to deploy new applications faster and turning security into a business risk to be managed, rather than a wall for IT to maintain.[10]

build a portfolio of cloud services to accelerate HERO projects

Cloud computing services put technology power directly into the hands of HEROes and developers. Facebook and Twitter are cloud services. So is Google App Engine, the tool that Ben Hedrington harnessed at Best Buy to build Twelpforce. So is Salesforce.com, the tool that Ross Inglis at Thomson Reuters used to launch the independent advisor product.

IT needs to know two things about cloud services. First, they are here to stay. The economic drivers of cloud computing—running at massive scale using highly automated systems—means lower costs and faster deployments. It's cheaper for entrepreneurs and developers to build new applications as (and on) a cloud computing service than as installed software.

Second, developers and HEROes will always look for the easiest way to get something done. And that means using a cloud service. There are

FIGURE 13-2

Cloud computing service categories

Cloud category	Description	Key vendors
Software as a service (SaaS)	These are configurable applications available as a service over the Internet. As a category, SaaS applications support a huge variety of business activities, from customer service to collaboration to compliance reporting.	• Cisco WebEx • Google Apps • IBM LotusLive.com • Microsoft Exchange Online • Salesforce.com
Platform as a service (PaaS)	These are service platforms for developers to build and operate new applications. With platform as a service, developers can launch a new application in weeks using a credit card to get started.	• Google App Engine • IBM Impact • Microsoft Azure • Salesforce Force.com
Infrastructure as a service (IaaS)	These are computers and storage running in a service providers' data center and available as an on-demand utility. These services allow IT to launch apps quickly, scale them up as needed, and pay for only the capacity used.	• Amazon Elastic Compute Cloud • AT&T Synaptic Compute & Storage • Rackspace • Terremark

three categories of cloud services: software, platform, and infrastructure. Each has its own place in the computing stack and solves different problems (see figure 13-2). In all three categories, it's easier to get started with a cloud service immediately than to write a business plan with a three-year breakeven just to get in line for funding.

IT groups should implement a strategy for cloud computing that makes it easier for HEROes and developers to use cloud services that IT can support. The goal is to avoid service redundancy and risky service providers. That strategy has four parts.

First, keep an eye on the cloud computing services that your employees and developers are using. Use a Web monitoring tool like WebSense or McAfee/Secure Computing to keep track of new cloud services being used by employees.[11] Establish a regular cadence of analyzing that data and maintaining an ever-growing list of cloud services to evaluate.

Second, identify a core set of services to support.[12] Create an evaluation process to assess the services and their competitors. Be sure to consider the complications of relying on some other company to run your core application. In Ben Hedrington's words, "Google App Engine is good for Twelpforce because if it goes down for an hour, our business will keep running." That may be true for Twelpforce, but it's certainly not true for BestBuy.com. When IT sourcing and vendor management teams assess cloud services, they need to understand the different needs of different classes of HERO projects and business-critical applications.

Third, implement the security and data integration needed. This can be hard, but it's where your IT enterprise architects, application developers, and infrastructure and operations professionals can help.

Fourth, get the word out to people in the business on the cloud services that you support. Here's a chance to use that collaboration system to make potential HEROes aware of what services are available and get feedback on how they're using it.

from corporate to personal

Now you know what IT needs to do to make HEROes successful. It's a transformation in IT roles, from operating isolated technology systems to supporting ubiquitous business technology—a completely new way of looking at technology in the corporate world.

At this point you may be wondering—what does a company that has done all this look like? How do I know where my company is on this transformative voyage? And what can I, personally, do to advance the ideals of a HERO-powered business in a corporation that hasn't yet adopted these changes?

We describe all of that in chapter 14, our last word on the subject of living in a HERO-powered business.

14. becoming HERO-powered

Finding a financial advisor is sort of like dating. You have to get to know someone and see if he or she thinks like you.

But there's only one financial institution that *treats* the relationship with financial advisors like dating: Canada's Sun Life Financial. If you're Canadian, you can go to www.sunlife.ca, tell them a little about yourself in a lively and cleverly designed Web application, and then check out the photos of some advisors whom you might find compatible. Just like on a dating site, you can check them out before you share your information.

This is a pretty wacky idea for a 145-year-old financial services company with more than fourteen thousand employees. But Sun Life isn't what it used to be. And the changes came about because of a change in attitude among all three groups in the HERO Compact—HEROes, IT, and management.

To understand where the change came from, start with management. Sun Life has operations in twenty-four countries and sells everything from pension plans for big corporate clients to life insurance for individuals. Inevitably, the organization had become siloed around geographies and products. There was a lot of duplication of effort.

New executives came in and wanted to change that. The CEO wanted to leverage the company's strength internationally, so geographies could learn from each other's experiences. The CMO wanted to create more awareness of Sun Life as a financial brand. And the CIO wanted to find ways for IT to add value to the business and stimulate innovation.

These changes in strategy energized two HEROes in Canada. Bill McCollam, whom we mentioned briefly in chapter 13, was vice president of digital strategy in Sun Life's marketing group. Tom Anger was in IT. Together, they gathered support for the idea that an international collaboration suite could get the management what it was looking for—innovation across geographies.

One outcome of this was IdeaShare, a three-month contest to get the best employee ideas around the globe. IdeaShare, much like Chubb's Imaginatik system that we described in chapter 10, is designed to get employees generating and commenting on each others' ideas. But the real challenge was getting Sun Life's far-flung staffers to participate. As we described in chapter 11, a viral video led to robust participation and more than two hundred fifty new ideas. These included improvements in the way customers get authenticated when calling the company and a new push to enable more online communication and less paperwork in dealings with customers. Another outcome was broader awareness and participation in Sun Life's internal collaboration tools, for which the usage is now growing at 10 percent per month.

What's more important than the sharing application is the change in Sun Life. Management now believes that innovation and collaboration will make the company more competitive, while IT and marketing work together closely, especially Tom and Bill. So closely, in fact, that Tom's technology responsibility has been moved, and he's now part of the marketing department, working directly with Bill's group.

What is it like to work in a HERO-powered business like Sun Life? I'll let Bill and Tom tell you themselves:

Bill: "The mandate at my group was to bring business units together on behalf of the customer. We will be working together a lot more. We integrate the [management] news on the intranet with the collaboration environment; it's not two distinct destinations. We Twitter jobs and use LinkedIn for recruiting. We are using these [social] tools internally and externally."

Tom: "This was not a traditional project where you spend two years and hope it meets your needs. We need to be constantly agile and evolve. Not be afraid to try—fail fast and fail often. Get the applications out there, get feedback, further investigate how best to roll it out. There is no point when we are going to say we are done. Social media is the dialtone of the twenty-first century."

is your company like Sun Life?

The changes at Sun Life took years to get going. Embracing HERO-powered innovation is hard, progress takes time, and the journey is never complete.

As you've read about Sun Life, Best Buy, IBM, and all the other model companies we've described, you've probably asked yourself two questions:

- How do I know if my company is getting closer to the HERO-powered ideal?

- What do I do when my company isn't there yet?

We'll answer those questions now.

how do I know if my company is getting closer to the HERO-powered ideal?

Most people just try to get their jobs done. Most managers would like to serve customers and run things efficiently. This discipline of customer-focused innovation doesn't come up every day, and it doesn't affect every employee. But when it does come up, it can make a dramatic difference in how it feels to work somewhere, because innovation is in the air. For regular workers, it just provides hope that they may be able to contribute in innovative ways—and without getting tangled in bureaucracy.

It helps to have signposts that reveal just how far along the journey you've come. Whether you're a worker with an idea, a manager, or an IT professional, here are some of the things that will tell you if the HERO-powered ideal is catching on with your company.

- *Ideas from HEROes are visible and recognized.* Think about innovations that caught on in your company. Who came up with them? Did the company recognize them? At BAE Systems, the company rewards HEROes with the Chairman's Award. At Comcast, customer-service HEROes get a Bowtie Award in honor of company founder Ralph Roberts. Companies well along the HERO-powered journey make HEROes visible and recognize their contributions as a way to provide motivation to others with similar ideas.

- *People are highly visible within sharing systems.* Your intranet may be shiny and pretty, but is anyone contributing? Many, many sharing systems are so barren and lifeless, you can almost hear the wind whistling past and see tumbleweeds blowing by. Innovation pretty much requires collaboration. If a wide variety of contributors is using your collaboration systems, your company is likely to be much more hospitable to HEROes.

- *Relationships frequently cross departmental boundaries.* Whom do you work with most frequently? If it's people within your own department—and if the company works that way—then your organization is probably set up so that innovation can take place only on your own turf. HEROes focus on customers, not just what benefits their department. If, on the other hand, you're often collaborating across boundaries, you're much more likely to get the support you need—and generate the ideas you need—to be a HERO.

- *Employees speak to customers.* An executive at a large technology company asked us if the company should use Twitter. Then he revealed that every press release has to go up and down five levels of management. Oops. This is clearly a company where employees do not regularly engage with customers in a public setting. Customer-focused innovation comes from actual customer engagement. If public engagement is strictly limited at your company, don't be surprised if customer-focused innovation isn't bubbling up all over.

- *Internal and external technologies seem parallel.* Employees often draw ideas from their external interactions and apply them internally—and vice versa. Do you put product demos up on an internal "YouTube"? Does your internal profile system mimic Facebook? Do you Yammer the way you Twitter? And conversely, are you making mobile apps based on corporate information available to customers because you did the same for workers? Have you turned your idea contests outward and invited customers to make suggestions? In HERO-powered businesses, this internal-external crossover is common.

- *IT and lines of business have a supportive relationship.* If you're not in IT, imagine going to your IT folks and asking for help with a technology project. How would they react? If you're in IT, how would you react? If the answer is, IT would try to help, would recommend vendors and technologies, and would advise on how the project could be completed safely, then your HEROes have a chance of succeeding. But if IT blocks or ignores these projects, it's going to be hard for HEROes to get anything done.

In the preceding chapters, we've delivered lots of advice on how companies can support HERO-powered innovation. But progress comes one step, one HERO, and one project at a time. That's why it's so important to build a HERO project or two, even if you're at the very beginning of this corporate transformation.

what do I do if my company isn't there yet?

Realistically, most companies are at the start of the journey toward empowering their HEROes. Don't wait for your company to change. Create the change yourself. While the top management of a company can accelerate the HERO-powered transformation, change can come from anywhere. HEROes, managers, and IT staff can contribute best by creating small successes, then building on them.

HEROes should build on small successes

If you're a creative staffer in touch with customers' needs, you can still be a HERO, even if your company isn't set up to reward it, yet. Managers are more likely to support you if you're productive, so follow the advice here in addition to, not instead of, performing your regular job.

First, spend some time learning how mobile, video, cloud, and social technologies work. If using your work computer for these purposes is prohibited, use a home computer. Depending on your skills, learn by connecting on YouTube or Twitter, making or uploading videos, perusing iPhone apps, and finding or even coding creative Web services.

Second, don't just identify customer problems, imagine solutions. What would you want if you were a customer? How can your sales, support, or marketing staff be more efficient? What solutions could you create?

Third, reach out to people who can help. While your peers may seem the most obvious, you may learn more from people in adjacent departments; salespeople can learn from support staff, for example, and marketing people from IT staff. If your company has collaboration systems, use them to pose questions or connect with people across departments. At this point, it's a good idea to let your boss know what you're imagining—depending on your relationship and the quality of your idea, he may help you, suggest productive directions, be indifferent, or even attempt to block your efforts, but it's better to know up front.

Fourth, build a plan. Use the Effort-Value Evaluation in chapter 2, not just to determine what class of project you're considering, but what sorts of challenges you may face. Your plan should include details on what resources you'll need, what allies are working with you, what sort of value you can produce, and how you can measure that value.

If your project affects customers or employees, you'll generally need some management approval—but you'll have to balance the need to get approvals higher up in the organization with the ability to get started. Depending on your level of daring, sometimes it's better to ask forgiveness than permission.

And don't stop at one project. If you succeed, you owe it to yourself and your company to find ways to extend that success. Successful HEROes often create new job descriptions and end up running groups dedicated to new kinds of solutions.

managers should encourage HERO efforts as visibly as possible

If you run a group or a department, how can you start the journey of becoming a HERO-powered business? You may be asking, "Why aren't my staff more creative problem solvers?" The answer, most likely, is that they don't get rewarded for taking risks. Here are some suggestions on how to change things.

First, start by hiring energetic and creative people. Hire for attitude as well as skills. Look for people who can build Web sites or shoot videos, or who have extensive social technology skills, perhaps from college or hobbies. These people are the most likely to be able to come up with customer-facing groundswell ideas.

Second, encourage people in any way possible. Creative use of technology is a spark; fan it into a flame. At General Mills, the marketing leadership holds monthly meetings of its department and highlights creative strategies used by other brands and industries; exposing your staff to new technologies and strategies is a best practice. Help potential HEROes by identifying them, encouraging their ideas, and recommending positive directions for change. Recognize innovative technology solutions with awards and public attaboys.

Third, participate yourself. You reached your position because you solve problems and find creative solutions. Once in a management position, don't lose your involvement. Contribute to the ideas, provide guidance on the kinds of ideas you can support, read the comments and rankings of others—even if it hurts.

Finally, help take concepts from idea to project to completion. You can do this by identifying other managers who can contribute, connecting HEROes with others who have similar interests, and running interference with other departments that may have problems. And if you want your HEROes to keep producing, don't take credit for their ideas. (Managers we spoke with during the research for this book were delighted to give credit to others who generated or contributed to HERO projects.)

Throughout all this activity, it's a good idea for managers in customer-facing departments to find sympathetic IT staff who are willing to provide advice and support, rather than those more likely to shut down projects.

As long as we're talking about management, here's a word for senior managers and CEOs: wondering why your people aren't more innovative? As we saw from so many managers in chapter 9, you have to learn to tolerate some failures to make innovation happen. The body language that senior managers project, especially during difficult economic times, has a lot of influence on HEROes' willingness to innovate. So does the way you support collaboration and innovation systems within your company.

IT staff must find ways to support HERO projects

How does an IT professional start down the path to a HERO-powered business? By taking one giant step toward the real customers of your company and the colleagues that serve them. Focusing on internal customers is fine to a point, but supporting HERO projects means understanding what customers need. This can be a tough transition for a highly technical person more comfortable with code books and procedures than handshakes and relationships. Here are some ways to do it better.

First, upgrade your customer skills by talking to people who work with customers every day. Go ahead, make that call to a marketing colleague, accept that brown bag lunch describing the new social strategy, stop by the desk of a technical liaison in the customer service organization. It starts with personal relationships with colleagues, but it doesn't need to stop there. Take an accounting class or attend a marketing seminar. It's all accessible to a curious technical person.

Second, focus more on making things better for customers and employees and perhaps less on trying to bulletproof and lock down systems. Take a little more risk so that HERO employees ask for your support rather than keeping things from you. In the words of Malcolm Harkins, chief information security officer at Intel, "Run toward the risk so you can shape it." That means knowing what's going on and finding ways to improve it.

Third, stake your claim as the company's technology expert. You're probably more enthusiastic about Android phones and HD video cameras than your average salesperson or product development manager. Showcase your talent and ideas. Wear your geek cloak with pride. Be the expert on all things groundswell. Bring your own experiences and experiment with radically new solutions to old problems.

Finally, don't be afraid that blue-collar IT jobs are disappearing. Be focused on happy customers and empowered HEROes, not applying software patches or testing maintenance fixes on old applications. If your job feels like a dead end in a world moving to the cloud, then make a change. Learn a new skill. Take a night class. Up your game so you become the technology expert in your HERO-powered business.

the journey is worth it

HEROes face great challenges in any company, and yet thousands have succeeded. You don't have to work for Sun Life to be a successful HERO.

They do it because it's impossible for any empowered, resourceful businessperson to see customers—or coworkers—in need and not ask, "Could we serve them better?"

They do it because, immersed in the same technologies as consumers, they wonder how those tools might be used in their jobs.

They do it because doing the same job as yesterday, with the same tools as yesterday, coloring only within the lines, is boring. And because they worry that that sort of complacency will leave them vulnerable to the whims of their own empowered customers.

They even do it because their company encourages HERO activity, provides the tools for it, and recognizes the ability HEROes have to inspire their colleagues.

Empowering more people in your organization is a force for good. It attracts smart people. It makes creative problem solving everybody's job. And it makes your company a more upbeat, enjoyable, and creative place to be.

Give yourself and your workers a chance to turn powerful technologies into machines that generate happy customers who talk about you. In the twenty-first century, this may be the only sustainable advantage you've got.

notes

When using these notes, keep in mind the following:

- To see sites cited in these footnotes, you don't need to enter long, complicated Web addresses. To simplify your access to these sites, we put them all into an online Delicious account. You can see all the site links with descriptions and tags by going to http://delicious.com/empowerednotes. To see all the notes for a given chapter, find the space labeled "Type a tag" and enter a chapter number with no space (for example, "chapter10"), then click on the arrow. You can get the same result by extending the Delicious Web address with the chapter number (for example, http://delicious.com/empowerednotes/chapter10). Similarly, you can find all the links for notes regarding a topic by using the tag for that topic (for example, "customerservice") or all the links regarding a company by typing the tag for the company name (for example, "Intuit").
- When a note references a Forrester report, only current Forrester clients can see the full report. Others viewing the report's Web address will see an abstract of the report.
- Regarding data: Most of the consumer and workforce data cited here comes from Forrester's North American Technographics Empowerment Online Survey, Q4 2009 (The base is U.S. online consumers (in chapters 1 through 6) or information workers (in chapters 7 through 14), unless otherwise indicated. Forrester conducted this survey in November 2009, reaching 10,111 U.S. individuals aged 18 to 88. For results based on a randomly chosen sample of this size (N = 10,111), there is 95% confidence that the results have a statistical precision of plus or minus 1% of what they would be if the entire population of U.S. online individuals aged 18 and older had been surveyed. Forrester weighted the data by age, gender, income, broadband adoption, and

region to demographically represent the adult U.S. online population. The survey sample size, when weighted, was 10,044. (Weighted sample sizes can be different from the actual number of respondents to account for individuals generally underrepresented in online panels.) Please note that this was an online survey. Respondents who participate in online surveys in general have more experience with the Internet and feel more comfortable transacting online. The data is weighted to be representative for the total online population on the weighting targets mentioned, but this sample bias may produce results that differ from Forrester's offline benchmark survey. The sample was drawn from members of MarketTools's online panel, and respondents were motivated by receiving points that could be redeemed for a reward. The sample provided by MarketTools is not a random sample. While individuals were randomly sampled from the MarketTools panel for this particular survey, they had previously chosen to take part in the MarketTools online panel.

chapter 1

1. *Her rant about the Maytag, titled "Containing a capital letter or two"*: See Heather Armstrong's August 28, 2009, blog post "Containing a capital letter or two" on the blog Dooce, http://www.dooce.com/2009/08/28/containing-capital-letter-or-two.

2. *Her book about mothering and postpartum depression*: *It Sucked and Then I Cried: How I Had a Baby, a Breakdown, and a Much Needed Margarita* by Heather Armstrong (Simon Spotlight Entertainment, 2009). Heather will also be appearing soon in a show on the HGTV cable channel.

3. *Whirlpool monitors social media*: Whirlpool told us it now has a "digital detectives" program and often responds to people it detects in social applications like Twitter who are having problems. It also has Twitter accounts for various brands, including @GladiatorGW, @JennAirUSA, @KitchenAidUSA, and @AmanaStyle. In February of 2010, several months after the problems Heather Armstrong had, it added the @MaytagCare Twitter account. The company has also changed its policy with regard to Twitter responses and now responds publicly in social channels rather than just trying to connect with people in private channels like email and telephone. For an example of Whirlpool's current social outreach, see Laura Northrop's February 10, 2010, blog post "Facebook and Twitter Complaint Gets Dead Whirlpool Oven Fixed" on the blog The Consumerist, http://consumerist.com/2010/02/facebook-and-twitter-complaint-gets-dead-whirlpool-oven-fixed.html.

4. Forbes *writes a story about it*: "A Twitterati Calls Out Whirlpool" by Parmy Olson, *Forbes*, September 2, 2009, http://www.forbes.com/2009/09/02/twitter-dooce-maytag-markets-equities-whirlpool.html.

5. *When Sacha Baron Cohen's* Brüno *came out, ticket sales on the first weekend were already dropping on Saturday and Sunday*: According to Infegy's Social Radar, negative buzz around *Brüno* was evident and could be responsible for the quick decline between Friday and Saturday of its opening weekend. See Eric's July 15, 2009, blog post "Twitter enabled negative word-of-mouth to instantly affect Bruno at the box office" on the blog Buzz Study, http://infegy.com/buzzstudy/ twitter-enabled-negative-word-of-mouth-to-instantly-affect-bruno-at-the-box-office/.

6. *Three out of four consumers in America and four out of five in Western Europe have a mobile phone*: See the Forrester report "US Mobile Forecast, 2009 to 2014" by Charles S. Golvin, November 6, 2009, http://www.forrester.com/rb/Research/ us_mobile_forecast%2C_2009_to_2014/q/id/53737/t/2.

7. *By 2009, 17 percent of the adult population, both in the United States and in Western Europe, already had mobile Internet service*: See the Forrester report "Western European Mobile Forecast, 2009 to 2014" by Thomas Husson, August 28, 2009, http://www.forrester.com/rb/Research/western_european_mobile_forecast %2C_2009_to_2014/q/id/53717/t/2.

8. *In one month in 2009, according to Comscore, 100 million Americans watched a total of 6 billion YouTube videos*: Comscore press release, "YouTube Surpasses 100 Million U.S. Viewers for the First Time," March 4, 2009, http://www.comscore.com/ layout/set/popup/Press_Events/Press_Releases/2009/3/YouTube_Sur passes_100_Million_US_Viewers.

9. *Cisco says that in 2008 video represented 21 percent of all the data flowing over the Internet, and estimates that will reach 91 percent by 2013*: "Cisco Visual Networking Index: Forecast and Methodology, 2008-2013," June 9, 2009, http:// www.cisco.com/en/US/solutions/collateral/ns341/ns525/ns537/ns705/ns827/white_ paper_c11-481360_ns827_Networking_Solutions_White_Paper.html.

10. *Four hundred thousand people viewed a video of then-U.S. Senator George Allen's use of the obscure racial epithet* macaca *to refer to a campaign worker*: See "George Allen introduces Macaca," August 15, 2006, on YouTube at http://www.youtube.com/watch?v=r90z0PMnKwI .

11. *Even the Realize Gastric Band, a surgically implanted device for obesity treatment, has its own YouTube channel*: http://www.youtube.com/user/Realize Band.

12. *When Derek Gottfrid needed raw computing power to process terabytes of digitized images for the* New York Times's *"Times Machine" archive, he just rented computing time on Amazon's EC2 servers*: See See Derek Gottfrid's May 21, 2008, blog post "The New York Times Archive + Amazon Web Services = Times-Machine" on the blog Open: All the Code That's Fit to printf(), http:// open.blogs.nytimes.com/2008/05/21/the-new-york-times-archives-amazon-web-services-timesmachine/.

13. *In the United States at the end of 2009, 59 percent of all online consumers were in social networks*: See the Forrester report "Introducing the New Social Technographics" by Josh Bernoff, January 15, 2010, http://www.forrester.com/rb/Research/ intro ducing_new_social_technographics%26%23174%3B/q/id/56291/t/2.

14. *In some places, like South Korea, three out of four online consumers connect with social content at least once a month*: Information available in the Groundswell Consumer Profile Tool at http://www.forrester.com/Groundswell/profile_tool.html.

chapter 2

1. *Veteran employee of Black and Decker*: The content of this case study refers to activities at Black & Decker before the completion of its merger with The Stanley Works on March 12, 2010. The merged company may pursue a different strategy. See www.stanleyblackanddecker.com.

2. *The CO.NX Facebook page*: See http://www.facebook.com/pages/Co Nx-See-the-World/26365096875.

3. *She hired developers to create an online community called Africa Rural Connect*: See http://www.AfricaRuralConnect.org/.

chapter 3

1. *The base of Dave's $3,500 Taylor guitar was smashed*: While there are hundreds of articles about Dave Carroll, you can read his first person account on his Web site: http://www.davecarrollmusic.com/story/united-breaks-guitars.

2. *He wrote a song called "United Breaks Guitars," spent $150 to make a video for it with his band, and loaded the video onto YouTube in July of 2009*: See http:// www.youtube.com/watch?v=5YGc4zOqozo.

3. *He's schmoozed with Whoopi Goldberg on* The View: See http://www. youtube.com/watch?v=SzzSYsL7nUE.

4. *A spike in social chatter about United Airlines just after "United Breaks Guitars" went live, especially on Twitter*: At our request, Sysomos provided a custom analysis of sentiment about United Airlines including the months before and after "United Breaks Guitars" debuted on YouTube. We gratefully acknowledge their help.

5. *At Forrester, we surveyed ten thousand people at the end of 2009*: All the Forrester numbers in this chapter come from Forrester's North American Technographics Empowerment Online Survey, Q4 2009 (US).

6. *Here's what we found*: Since all the numbers in this chapter are based on an estimate of the online population, we should be clear about how we define online adults. Our surveys are representative of the civilian, noninstitutionalized, non-group-quarters population in the continental United States for people eighteen and older. This information is derived from the March 2008 supplement of the Current Population Survey (CPS) of the U.S. Census. We identify a person as an

online adult if they say they go online at least once a month from home, at work, at school, or elsewhere.

7. *Within social networks, consumers create 256 billion impressions on one another by talking about products and service each year:* Here's how we compute this number. In our online survey, we ask which social networks respondents belong to, how many friends, followers, or connections they have in those networks, and how frequently they post about products or services in those places. Each individual then gets a "peer influence score" based on the number of impressions they create about products and services in a year in all social networks. We sum those impressions to get a total number of influence impressions for the whole sample. We then project the sample out to the whole population of online adults in the United States, which, based on our other surveys in 2009, we estimate at 176 million.

8. *In social environments like blogs and discussion forums and on sites that feature ratings and reviews, customers generate 1.64 billion posts:* Here's how we calculate this number. In our online survey, we ask how frequently respondents post about products and services in blogs, blog comments, discussion forums, and rating and review sites. Each individual then gets a "content influence score" based on the number of posts he or she makes in a year on all of these types of sites. We sum those numbers to get a total number of influence posts for the whole sample. We then project the sample out to the whole population of online adults in the United States, which, based on our other surveys in 2009, we estimate at 176 million.

9. *According to Nielsen Online, advertisers delivered 1.974 trillion online ad impressions in the twelve months ending in September 2009, the time period covered by our survey:* Nielsen Online provided us with this number based on their analysis of online advertising impressions for the twelve months ending September 30, 2009.

10. *In 2000, Malcolm Gladwell wrote an incredibly insightful book called* The Tipping Point: *The Tipping Point: How Little Things Can Make a Big Difference* (Little, Brown, 2000), http://www.gladwell.com/tippingpoint/index.html.

11. *80 percent of the influence comes from 20 percent of the consumers:* The 80-20 rule is often referred to as the Pareto principle.

12. *Daniel Grozdich is a working-class comedian in Malibu, California:* These descriptions come from the Fiesta Movement Web site at http://chapter1.fiesta movement.com/agents/.

13. *In 2009, 73 percent of online consumers aged 18 to 24 were using social content at least once a month:* We computed the Social Technographics Profile of consumers in different age groups. (For information about this profile, see *Groundswell.*) See the Forrester report "Introducing the New Social Technographics" by Josh Bernoff, January 15, 2010, http://www.forrester.com/rb/Research/introducing_ new_social_technographics&%23174%3B/q/id/56291/t/2.

14. *Enough outreach like this will create a customer who broadcasts your praises:* This idea has become popular lately. Joseph Jaffe even wrote a book about it: *Flip*

the Funnel: How to Use Existing Customers to Gain New Ones (Wiley, 2010). See Joseph Jaffe's February 7, 2010, blog post "Flip the Funnel: Halve Your Budget; Double Your Revenue" on the blog Jaffe Juice, http://www.jaffejuice.com/2010/02/flip-the-funnel-halve-your-budget-double-your-revenues.html.

15. *When they sent me the most deliciously tempting newsletter I've ever read, I blogged it*: See Josh Bernoff's blog posts "The best email marketing I ever got" (April 19, 2007) and "Rentvillas.com shows how to be a human" (December 22, 2008) on the blog Groundswell, http://blogs.forrester.com/groundswell/2007/04/the_best_email_.html and http://blogs.forrester.com/groundswell/2008/12/rentvillas com-s.html.

chapter 4

1. *Among major operators, Comcast was at the bottom*: See the Forrester report "Satellite Still Leads Cable In Satisfaction" by Josh Bernoff, March 4, 2004, http://www.forrester.com/rb/Research/satellite_still_leads_cable_in_satisfaction/q/id/33986/t/2.

2. *A video of a technician who'd come to fix a customer's cable modem, then fell asleep on his couch, racked up over a million views on YouTube*: Brian Finkelstein, who also created "Snakes on a Blog," posted this video. It's had a sordid history. We cited it in *Groundswell* and it's also been cited in many other social media books, blogs, and discussions. The video was removed from YouTube for a while, apparently due to a copyright complaint from the owner of the music used in the video. It has now been restored, but not by the same user, and includes a link to buy the music: http://www.youtube.com/watch?v=CvVp7b5gzqU.

3. *Bob Garfield started a blog for Comcast complainers, comcastmustdie.com, and gathered 191 comments on his very first post*: See Bob Garfield's October 4, 2007, blog post "How to Use This Blog" on the blog Comcast Must Die, http://comcastmustdie.blogspot.com/2007/10/how-to-use-this-blog.html.

4. *As reported in the* Washington Post, *Mona Shaw, a seventy-five-year-old Virginia grandmother, became so frustrated with ongoing service interruptions that she went down to the local cable office with a claw hammer and smashed every bit of equipment in sight*: The article included a nice photo of Mona and her hammer. See "Taking a Whack Against Comcast" by Neely Tucker, *Washington Post*, October 18, 2007, http://www.washingtonpost.com/wp-dyn/content/article/2007/10/17/AR2007101702359.html.

5. *They focused only on efficiency and forgot about the value of the customer experience*: See the Forrester report "Best Practices: Five Strategies For Customer Service Social Media Excellence" by Natalie L. Petouhoff, August 14, 2009, http://www.forrester.com/rb/Research/best_practices_five_strategies_for_customer_service/q/id/48001/t/2.

6. *Take this one, from a customer going by "R. Pink Floyd"*: http://www. ama zon. com/review/R2GK2AEW8BOATJ/ref=cm_cr_pr_viewpnt#R2GK2AEW8 BOATJ.

7. *The companywide transformation that comes from embracing social technologies in everything from marketing to product innovation*: See Josh Bernoff's October 29, 2008, blog post "2008 Forrester Groundswell Award Winners" on the blog Groundswell, http://blogs.forrester.com/groundswell/2008/10/2008-forrester.html.

8. *The community forums for FICO*: See http://ficoforums.myfico.com/fico/.

9. *Here are the company's core values, developed by the employees themselves and used in evaluating hires*: See http://about.zappos.com/jobs/why-work-zappos/ our-ten-core-values

10. *Naturally, Wendy blogged about Zappos again*: See Wendy Fitch's September 14, 2009, blog post "That darn Zappos.com" on the blog "The Honeymoon Is Over," http://decembertenth2005.blogspot.com/2009/09/that-darn-zapposcom .html.

chapter 5

1. *E*TRADE Mobile Pro is now an essential part of the company's strategy*: See the Forrester report "Case Study: E*TRADE Leverages Mobile To Offer Customers More Convenient Services" by Julie A. Ask, May 27, 2009, http:// www.forrester.com/rb/Research/case_study_etrade_leverages_mobile_to_offer/q /id/54567/t/2.

2. *In 2009, 34 million U.S. consumers used mobile phones to access the Internet; Forrester forecasts that number will reach 106 million by 2014*: See the Forrester report "US Mobile Forecast, 2009 To 2014" by Charles S. Golvin, November 6, 2009, http://www.forrester.com/rb/Research/us_mobile_forecast%2C_2009_to_2014/ q/id/53737/t/2.

3. *In Western Europe, we expect mobile Internet penetration to reach 39 percent of mobile phone owners by 2014*: See the Forrester report "Western European Mobile Forecast, 2009 To 2014" by Thomas Husson, August 28, 2009, http://www. forrester.com/rb/Research/western_european_mobile_forecast%2C_2009_to_20 14/q/id/53717/t/2.

4. *Our analysis of successful mobile applications shows that the best empower customers with immediacy, simplicity, and context*: See the Forrester report "The Convenience Quotient Of Mobile Services: A Facebook Case Study" by Julie A. Ask, October 14, 2009, http://www.forrester.com/rb/Research/convenience_quotient_ of_mobile_services_facebook_case/q/id/53682/t/2

5. *Examine the people and objectives first, before designing a strategy and choosing a technology*: See the Forrester report "The POST Method: A Systematic Approach To Mobile Strategy" by Julie A. Ask and Charles S. Golvin, April 9, 2009,

http://www.forrester.com/rb/Research/post_method_systematic_approach_to_mobile_strategy/q/id/53677/t/2.

6. *Nationwide Insurance built an iPhone app that walks its policyholders through the process of preparing to file a claim right at the scene of an accident*: See the Forrester report "Case Study: Nationwide Insurance Uses Mobile To Offer Customers Self Service On The Road" by Julie A. Ask, September 11, 2009, http://www.forrester.com/rb/Research/case_study_nationwide_insurance_uses_mobile_to/q/id/55230/t/2.

7. *UPS is the world's largest shipping company, delivering 15 million packages every day*: http://www.pressroom.ups.com/Fact+Sheets/UPS+Fact+Sheet.

8. *Make it available to that customer on any connected device*: When UPS released the iPhone app, it simultaneously upgraded the mobile site m.ups.com. Mobile site users can do shipping now, just like iPhone app users.

chapter 6

1. *Microsoft edited them together in short snippets to create a series of "I'm a PC" commercials*: That first "I'm a PC" commercial has racked up over 500,000 views on YouTube: http://www.youtube.com/watch?v=hi1se9rH7S8.

2. *All the social posts about Windows 7 from Twitter, Facebook, Blogs, YouTube, and Flickr into one highly dynamic site*: As we write this, the site is still available and includes 280,000 posts; 93% are from Twitter: http://www.microsoft.com/windows/social.

3. *A video with an ethnically mixed set of "typical" partygoers that comes off, shall we say, a little stilted and square*: See http://www.youtube.com/watch?v=1cX4t5-YpHQ.

4. *Like customer service, fan base cultivation is an activity that never ends*: Smart marketers are using social applications before, during, and after advertising campaigns, treating the fans they assemble as a long-term asset. See the Forrester report "Using Social Applications In Ad Campaigns" by Sean Corcoran, April 29, 2009, http://www.forrester.com/rb/Research/using_social_applications_in_ad_campaigns/q/id/54050/t/2.

5. *Choose a listening platform—a company that, for a fee, will help you monitor online commentary about your company and your products*: For a review and comparison of listening platforms, see the Forrester report "The Forrester Wave: Listening Platforms, Q1 2009" by Suresh Vittal, January 23, 2009, http://www.forrester.com/rb/Research/wave%26trade%3B_listening_platforms%2C_q1_2009/q/id/48093/t/2.

6. *Before this program, McNally Smith was mentioned in 2.7 percent of online conversations about music colleges; afterward, it was mentioned in 12.1 percent*: McNally Smith was a finalist for the Forrester Groundswell Awards in 2009. This information

is drawn from its entry for those awards. See http://www. groundswelldiscussion. com/groundswell/awards2009/detail.php?id=153.

7. *Is the one created by AMC for the TV series* Mad Men: AMC's *Mad Men* application was a finalist for the Forrester Groundswell Awards in 2009. This information is drawn from its entry for those awards. See http://www. groundswelldiscussion.com/groundswell/awards2009/detail.php?id=178.

8. *The most popular of more than two hundred fifty Coca-Cola fan pages on Facebook*: See "How Two Coke Fans Brought the Brand to Facebook Fame" by Abbey Klaassen, *Advertising Age,* March 16, 2009, http://adage.com/abstract.php? article_id=135238.

9. *Evian's video featuring break-dancing babies on roller skates*: At the time of this writing, this video has over 12 million views. See http://www.youtube. com/watch?v=_PHnRIn74Ag.

10. *Sonic Foundry, a technology vendor that sells Webcasts to corporations, is one company that turned this sort of concentration of messages to its advantage*: Sonic Foundry's Mediasite User Conference application won the Forrester Groundswell Award in the category of business-to-business energizing in 2009. This information is drawn from its entry for those awards. See http://www. groundswelldiscussion.com/groundswell/awards2009/detail.php?id=105.

11. *Norton's average ratings on those sites went from two stars to four and a half (on a five-point scale)*: Norton and Zuberance won the Forrester Groundswell Award in the category of business-to-consumer energizing in 2009. This information is drawn from personal interviews as well as the awards entry. See http://www.groundswelldiscussion.com/groundswell/awards2009/detail.php?id= 196.

12. *Counsel marketers to maintain authenticity in sourcing customer content*: One way of looking at marketing activity as the pursuit of three types of media: earned (fan word of mouth), owned (for example, your own site), and paid (for example, advertisements). Within "earned media," Forrester analyst Sean Corcoran makes a further distinction among three types of word of mouth: positive organic (unprompted and authentic word of mouth), brand stimulated (communication incented by a brand, like Zuberance's work with Norton), and spurned media (negative word of mouth from unhappy customers, like Dave "United Breaks Guitars" Carroll). See the Forrester report "No Media Should Stand Alone" by Sean Corcoran, December 16, 2009, http://www.forrester.com/rb/Research/no_ media_should_stand_alone/q/id/54869/t/2.

13. *The site saw a 1,332 percent increase in Web visitors, driven by news coverage, word of mouth, and curiosity*: See "Skittles Social Media Campaign Increases Traffic 1332% in One Day" by Andy Beal, March 9, 2009, http://www.marketing pilgrim.com/2009/03/skittles-social-media-campaign-increases-traffic-1332-in-one-day.html.

14. *The company conducted an online contest for watch designs in 2008, attracting more than nine hundred innovative designs*: See http://www.enlightened-watch-design-contest.com/index.php.

15. *The Starbucks site mystarbucksidea.com has now generated over eighty thousand ideas for the company, of which over fifty have been implemented*: See http://mystarbucksidea.force.com/.

16. *Intuit has recruited seventeen thousand people into its TurboTax Inner Circle; the company uses them as a sounding board for new tax preparation software ideas*: TurboTax Inner Circle was one of four Intuit applications that earned the company the Forrester Groundswell Award for Company Transformation in 2008. See http://www.forrester.com/Groundswell/embracing/turbotax_circle.html.

17. *The auto-racing organization NASCAR, taking cues from its twelve-thousand-member fan community, changed the rules for races*: The NASCAR Fan Council won the Forrester Groundswell Award in the business-to-consumer listening category in 2009. The information here was drawn from that awards entry. See http://www.groundswelldiscussion.com/groundswell/awards2009/detail.php?id=185.

18. *Using the hashtag #NHLTweetup*: Dani's Web site is visible at www.nhltweetup.com. It's not officially affiliated with the NHL and is a labor of love for Dani. Also see the Forrester report "Case Study: The NHL Uses Tweet-Ups To Energize Its Fan Base And Reach New Audiences" by Nate Elliott, November 4, 2009, http://www.forrester.com/rb/Research/case_study_nhl_uses_tweet-ups_to_energize/q/id/55321/t/2.

19. *The people at the New York tweetup had 21,336 followers, all of whom could be hearing about the hockey happening in New York, in real time*: "Success of Global 'Tweetup' Shows NHL's Embrace of Twitter" by Kevin Allen, *USA Today*, April 29, 2009, http://www.usatoday.com/sports/hockey/nhl/2009-04-29-twitter-tweetup-capitals-twackle_N.htm.

20. *"How To Create A Social Application For Life Sciences Without Getting Fired"*: See the Forrester report "How To Create A Social Application For Life Sciences Without Getting Fired" by Josh Bernoff, April 20, 2009, http://www.forrester.com/rb/Research/create_social_application_for_life_sciences_without/q/id/53435/t/2.

21. *Andy Sernovitz's book* Word of Mouth Marketing: *Word of Mouth Marketing: How Smart Companies Get People Talking, Revised Edition* by Andy Sernovitz (Kaplan Press, 2009). The author's blog, "Damn! I Wish I'd Thought of That," is available at http://damniwish.com.

chapter 7

1. *Here's how we told the story in* Groundswell: *Groundswell: Winning in a World Transformed by Social Technologies* by Charlene Li and Josh Bernoff (Harvard Business Press, 2008), p. 217.

2. *We needed a platform that could plug into those channels*: Taken from a video interview by Jason Falls. See Jason Falls's March 19, 2009, video and blog post "SME-TV: Discovering the Best Buy Blue Shirt Nation" on the blog Social Media Explorer, http://www.socialmediaexplorer.com/2009/03/19/sme-tv-discovering-the-best-buy-blue-shirt-nation/.

3. *We call this trend "technology populism"*: Technology populism—the adopting of consumer technologies in corporate settings—isn't completely new. For example, the original adoption of PCs inside of corporations came from the consumer side and created pressure on IT to support the new machines. See the Forrester report "Embracing the Risks and Rewards of Technology Populism" by Matthew Brown, Kyle McNabb, and Rob Koplowitz, February 22, 2008, http://www.forrester.com/rb/Research/embrace_risks_and_rewards_of_technology_populism/q/id/44664/t/2.

4. *Researchers at Computer Sciences Corporation (CSC) have called it the "consumerization of information technology"*: See http://lef.csc.com/library/publication detail.aspx?id=1220.

5. *As he told* Wired *magazine*: "My Greatest Mistake: Learn from Eight Luminaries" *Wired*, January 2010, http://www.wired.com/magazine/2009/12/fail_greatest_mistakes/.

chapter 8

1. *"But the challenge is they have already chosen the technology"*: We worked with PTC on a project to prepare the company for a customer community in 2009. As part of that project, we conducted interviews with key executives. Normally, interviews of this kind done in the context of a project are confidential and the property of the client (in this case, PTC). In 2010, PTC gave us permission to use this quote from Steve Horan, which came from the original set of stakeholder interviews.

2. *PTC's customers were overwhelmingly ready to embrace a community*: You can see the results of our survey for PTC on the company's blog. See Robin Saitz's June 5, 2009, blog post "Think Engineers and Web 2.0 Don't Mix? Think Again!" on the blog Social Product Development, http://social-product-develop ment.blogspot.com/2009/06/think-engineers-and-web-20-dont-mix.html.

chapter 9

1. *The small-business marketing group has innovated with its hyperlocal "Love a Local Business" feature*: See http://lovealocalbusiness.intuit.com/.

2. *Clayton Christensen describes this challenge in his book* The Innovator's Dilemma: *The Innovator's Dilemma: When New Technologies Cause Great Firms to Fail* by Clayton Christensen (Harvard Business School Press, 1997), http://www.claytonchristensen.com/books.html.

3. *As a result, Vail Resorts' CEO Rob Katz decided to change his marketing completely:* You can see Rob Katz describe the changes the company made in this video: http://adage.com/aboutdigital/article?article_id=140710.

4. *His followers and blog readers got to read about how great Vail is:* See Rob Lefsetz's November 28, 2009, blog post "Twitterific" on the blog The Lefsetz Letter, http://lefsetz.com/wordpress/index.php/archives/2009/11/28/twitterific/.

chapter 10

1. *Imaginatik is one of eleven different software systems that companies use to manage innovation:* See the Forrester report "Vendor Landscape: Innovation Management Software" by Matthew Brown, March 2, 2009, http://www.forrester.com/rb/Research/vendor_landscape_innovation_management_software/q/id/47927/t/2.

2. *Pete changed that:* In the small-world department, we were startled to realize that when we started talking with Pete about his work with Deloitte, we had already met him in a different context. He won a Forrester Groundswell Award in 2009 by using social technology for social good. When brushfires hit the town where he lived, he used blogs and video sharing to raise awareness and, eventually, over $1 million to help with the recovery: http://blogs.forrester.com/groundswell/2009/10/winners-of-the-2009-forrester-groundswell-awards.html.

3. *The original sixty people who had been testing Yammer grew to hundreds as over fifteen hundred tagline suggestions got posted over a twenty-four-hour period:* The final choice of the tagline was "Let's Go"—short, sweet, and a nice match to the company's green light logo. To hear Pete Williams talk about how Yammer caught on, see his December 16, 2009, blog post "How to Keep a Yammer Network Exploding" on the blog "Deloitte Digital," http://deloittedigital.blogspot.com/2009/12/how-to-keep-yammer-network-exploding.html.

chapter 11

1. *People from all around Intel can count on utility as they connect with the company's sharing tools, and on support when they build their own:* See the Forrester report "Case Study: Intel Implements People as the New Perimeter to Mitigate Social Computing Risks" by Khalid Kark, December 9, 2009, http://www.forrester.com/rb/Research/case_study_intel_implements_people_as_new/q/id/55840/t/2.

chapter 12

1. *Domino's still suffered brand damage:* See "Video Prank at Domino's Taints Brand" by Stephanie Clifford, *New York Times,* April 15, 2009, http://www.nytimes.com/2009/04/16/business/media/16dominos.html.

2. *Posted details about the Palm Pre phone on a blog, violating a nondisclosure agreement*: See the April 27, 2009, blog post "Some Palm Pre Questions" on the blog Inside Sprint Now, http://insidesprintnow.wordpress.com/2009/04/27/sprint-palm-pre-release-date-soon/.

3. *You can read it at Kodak.com*: See "Social Media Tips" from Jeff Hayzlett, chief marketing officer, vice president, Eastman Kodak Company, 2009, http://www.kodak.com/US/images/en/corp/aboutKodak/onlineToday/Social_Media_9_8.pdf.

4. *IBM's social computing guidelines include this statement*: See "IBM Social Computing Guidelines: Blogs, wikis, social networks, virtual worlds, and social media," http://www.ibm.com/blogs/zz/en/guidelines.html.

chapter 13

1. *Ben's idea was building an experimental Twitter aggregation service called ConnectTweet*: ConnectTweet is an application running on Google's App Engine cloud that uses Twitter's Web APIs to search for tweets with a particular hashtag and retweets them through a central Twitter name, in this case, through @twelpforce. Ben has said that people can contact him and run their own Twitter aggregation service. For more information about this tool, see Ben's blog at http://www.buildcontext.com/blog/ or the ConnectTweet home page at http://www.connecttweet.com/.

2. *We've been analyzing this "consumerization of IT" since 2008*: We first wrote about Technology Populism, our term for the Consumerization of IT, in the Forrester report "Embrace The Risks And Rewards Of Technology Populism" by Matthew Brown, Kyle McNabb, and Rob Koplowitz, February 22, 2008, http://www.forrester.com/rb/Research/embrace_risks_and_rewards_of_technology_populism/q/id/44664/t/2.

3. *He decided to give employees a choice of smartphones and PDAs*: We found three companies willing to share their experiences with iPhones as an enterprise productivity and collaboration tool. See the Forrester report "Making iPhone Work In The Enterprise: Early Lessons Learned" by Ted Schadler, April 10, 2009, http://www.forrester.com/rb/Research/making_iphone_work_in_enterprise_early_lessons/q/id/46634/t/2.

4. *IT should own the collaboration program*: See the Forrester report "Benchmarking Your Collaboration Strategy" by Rob Koplowitz and Ted Schadler, November 24, 2009, http://www.forrester.com/rb/Research/benchmarking_collaboration_strategy/q/id/48336/t/2.

5. *We have identified five anchor technologies that power many HERO projects*: For more on technologies that enterprise architects should track, see the Forrester report "The Top 15 Technology Trends EA Should Watch" by Alex Cullen, October 6, 2009, http://www.forrester.com/rb/Research/top_15_technology_trends_ea_should_watch/q/id/54322/t/2.

6. *This requires a new set of business intelligence and data-quality tools:* See the Forrester report "The Business Case For BI: Now More Critical Than Ever" by Boris Evelson, August 25, 2009, http://www.forrester.com/rb/Research/business_case_for_bi_now_more_critical/q/id/54955/t/2.

7. *Makes building a native mobile application for all phones an impossible task for most companies:* We are carefully monitoring the adoption of smartphones to help mobile application developers make the best decision on which platforms to support. See the Forrester report "The Mobile Architecture Imperative" by Jeffrey S. Hammond and Ellen Daley, August 1, 2008, http://www.forrester.com/rb/Research/mobile_architecture_imperative/q/id/42270/t/2.

8. *Led in our 2009 evaluation by Jive Software and Teligent:* See the Forrester report "The Forrester Wave: Community Platforms, Q1 2009" by Jeremiah K. Owyang, January 9, 2009, http://www.forrester.com/rb/Research/wave%26trade%3B_ community_platforms%2C_q1_2009/q/id/46468/t/2

9. *RESTful APIs are replacing older-style Web service interfaces:* Getting data in and out of databases in a way that works over the Internet is a challenge. After a decade of different approaches, one is gaining the support of every major cloud and application vendor. It's called the "representational state transfer" protocol, known to developers as REST or RESTful APIs. For background, see https://www.ibm.com/developerworks/webservices/library/ws-restful/.

10. *Turning security into a business risk to be managed, rather than a wall for IT to maintain:* See the Forrester report "Twelve Recommendations For Your 2010 Information Security Strategy" by Khalid Kark, January 11, 2010, http://www.forrester.com/rb/Research/twelve_recommendations_for_2010_information_security_strategy/q/id/56080/t/2.

11. *Keep track of new cloud services being used by employees:* For a comparison of Web filtering vendors, see the Forrester report "The Forrester Wave: Web Filtering, Q2 2009" by Chenxi Wang, April 16, 2009, http://www. forrester.com/rb/Research/wave%26trade%3B_web_filtering%2C_q2_2009/q/id/53897/t/2.

12. *Identify a core set of services to support:* For an evaluation of the maturity and relevance of cloud computing categories, see the Forrester report "TechRadar For Infrastructure & Operations Professionals: Cloud Computing, Q3 2009" by James Staten, October 2, 2009, http://www.forrester.com/rb/Research/techradar/%26trade%3B_for_infrastructure_%26_operations_professionals_cloud/q/id/54338/t/2.

acknowledgments

It was a challenge to create this book.

Because nobody had written a book about HEROes before, it took a while to get it all to come together. At times we felt like highly empowered and resourceful operatives ourselves, creating and exploring this idea within a busy, buzzing research company in the middle of a recession. I hope you liked the results. We'd love to tell you a little more about what it took to get here.

Three people in the management of Forrester Research made this book possible. George F. Colony, Forrester's founder and CEO, supported us in creating a book to follow *Groundswell* because he loves the power of ideas. Our COO, Charles Rutstein, suggested putting together our ideas on empowered consumers and empowered employees. That's what got us to HEROes, so thank you, Charles. And it was Forrester's CMO, Dwight Griesman, who supported this project from idea through publication and beyond. It's good to know your bosses have your back.

This book lives within a rich matrix of collaborators: the entire Forrester Research organization. We had the luxury of tapping into the ideas of Forrester's three hundred analysts and countless research and support staff. Among our analyst collaborators were Julie Ask, Matt Brown, Bobby Cameron, David Cooperstein, Sean Corcoran, Nate Elliott, Nigel Fenwick, Frank Gillett, Charles S. Golvin, Mike Gualtieri, Jeffrey Hammond, Liz Herbert, Khalid Kark, Rob Koplowitz, George Lawrie,

Sharyn Leaver, John McCarthy, Chris McLean, Sheri McLeish, Stephen Noble, Christine Overby, Natalie Petouhoff, Augie Ray, Clay Richardson, Emily Riley, James Staten, and Rob Whitely. We borrowed their insights shamelessly. We were fortunate to work with a brace of data experts, including Remy Fiorentino, Emily Van Metre, Cynthia Pflaum, Peter Schmidt, and Roxana Strohmenger. The clever Jennifer Wise did all the graphics, with design support from Jens Kueter. Amy Lewis and Corey Mathews turned our interaction ideas into a Web site; Phil LeClare, Karyl Levinson, Tracy Sullivan, and Jon Symons helped get our ideas out into the broader discussion in the media and on blogs; Michael Woodring managed this unmanageable project. We leaned on, begged resources from, and took inspiration from Forrester's research leadership, including Cliff Condon, Julie Meringer, Tom Pohlmann, and Dennis van Lingen. They held up the management end of our HERO Compact.

Our agent, Ike Williams, and editor, Jacque Murphy, made a second Forrester book happen: a clear demonstration of the triumph of hope over experience.

This book would not exist without the blind faith of Ted's family: Deirdre, Rory, and Sophie. As for Josh's family—Kimberley, Rachel, and Isaac—they knew what was coming, and still said yes. *Oy.*

Finally, this book is real because of the HEROes who allowed us to tell their stories. They came from everywhere—some were clients, some were famous, and some were just people who responded to Twitter requests—and helped us to see what it takes to be empowered and resourceful. Thanks for your persistence and the articulate way in which you described your experiences. Let's hope your efforts inspire HEROes throughout the world.

—Josh Bernoff and Ted Schadler
Cambridge, Massachusetts
March 2010

case indexes

Full case studies are in *italic*. Numbers indicate chapters.

cases and examples by industry

cases and examples by role

cases and examples by technology or application

index

about the authors

JOSH BERNOFF is Senior Vice President, Idea Development, at Forrester Research and is responsible for identifying, developing, and promoting some of the company's most influential and forward-looking ideas.

Josh is the coauthor of the *BusinessWeek* bestselling book *Groundswell: Winning in a World Transformed by Social Technologies* (Harvard Business Press, 2008), a comprehensive analysis of corporate strategy for dealing with social technologies. Abbey Klaassen of *Advertising Age* named it as the best book ever written on marketing and media, and Amazon's editors put it in the top ten business books of the year. In 2008, the Society for New Communications Research picked Josh and his *Groundswell* coauthor Charlene Li as "visionaries of the year."

Josh joined Forrester in 1995. In 1996 he created the Technographics segmentation, a classification of consumers according to how they approach technology. Forrester has used this segmentation as the basis of its consumer research offering, also called Technographics, since 1997. Josh is also known for his ten years of analysis of the television industry.

Josh's research, analysis, and opinions appear frequently in publications like the *New York Times* and the *Wall Street Journal*. He writes a column for *Marketing News,* a publication of the American Marketing Association, and blogs for Forrester and *Advertising Age*. Josh has keynoted major conferences on television, music, marketing, and technology in Barcelona, Cannes, Chicago, London, New York, Rome, São Paulo, and Tokyo.

TED SCHADLER is Vice President and Principal Analyst at Forrester Research. His work over thirteen years at Forrester has consistently focused on disruptive technologies and how senior decision makers should harness them. Ted uses quantitative studies and business analysis to identify and answer the technology questions of executives in business and consumer markets.

Since Ted joined Forrester in 1997, he has had a wide and varied career as an analyst, research director, innovator, and business manager. Ted has been instrumental in analyzing the impact of Internet 1.0, open source software, Web services, digital media, broadband, cloud computing, smartphones, and collaboration. In 2000, Ted launched and managed Forrester TechRankings, the precursor to the Forrester Wave methodology.

In 2009, Ted created Forrester's Workforce Technographics methodology, the industry's first benchmark analysis of how people use technology at work. This quantitative approach to understanding workforce technology has led to many of the ideas in *Empowered*.

Ted has appeared as a technology expert on ABC, CBC, CNBC, NBC, and PBS and his research and analysis has been cited in *BusinessWeek,* the *Economist,* the *New York Times,* and the *Wall Street Journal.* Ted has keynoted at business technology and marketing conferences worldwide.

Ted's background includes five years as a professional rock-and-roll musician for the Maryland-based band Crash Davenport, and ten years as Chief Technology Officer for a company building healthcare applications. He has degrees from Swarthmore College, the University of Maryland College Park, and MIT Sloan School of Business.